SECOND EDITION
Breakthroughs

An Integrated Advanced
English Program

Workbook

Marina Engelking

Gloria McPherson-Ramirez

OXFORD
UNIVERSITY PRESS

OXFORD
UNIVERSITY PRESS

8 Sampson Mews, Suite 204, Don Mills, Ontario M3C 0H5
www.oupcanada.com

Oxford University Press is a department of the University of Oxford.
It furthers the University's objective of excellence in research,
scholarship,and education by publishing worldwide in

Oxford   New York

Auckland   Cape Town   Dar es Salaam   Hong Kong   Karachi
Kuala Lumpur   Madrid   Melbourne   Mexico City   Nairobi
New Delhi   Shanghai   Taipei   Toronto

With offices in
Argentina   Austria   Brazil   Chile   Czech Republic   France   Greece
Guatemala   Hungary   Italy   Japan   Poland   Portugal   Singapore
South Korea   Switzerland   Thailand   Turkey   Ukraine   Vietnam

Oxford is a trade mark of Oxford University Press in the UK
and in certain other countries

Published in Canada
by Oxford University Press

Library and Archives Canada Cataloguing in Publication

Engelking, Marina, 1959-

   Breakthroughs. Workbook : an integrated advanced English program /
Marina Engelking, Gloria McPherson-Ramirez. — 2nd ed.

ISBN 978-0-19-542739-4

   1. English language—Problems, exercises, etc. 2. English language—
Textbooks for second language learners.

I. McPherson-Ramirez, Gloria, 1963– II. Title.

PE1112.E54 2007 Suppl. 1   428.2'4   C2008-902293-9

Printed on paper containing 40% post consumer waste
Printed and bound in Canada.

2 3 4 — 12 11 10

Contents

Unit 1
The Calm Before the Storm

Vocabulary

Exercise A

Rewrite each sentence below using one of the following words. Notice how the use of precise vocabulary eliminates the need for extra words and allows you to express the meaning of the sentences and the images they convey in a simpler way.

aftershocks	erupted	poisonous gases
blinding	eye	torrential
epicentre	fissures	twister

EXAMPLE: The rain, which was coming down extremely hard and fast, soaked Harold to the skin.

The torrential rain soaked Harold to the skin.

1. The snow was coming down so hard we couldn't see to drive, so we pulled off the road.

   _____

   _____

2. At 10:45 p.m. last night, lava shot out of the mouth of the volcano.

   _____

   _____

3. A swirling circle of air current touched down and destroyed everything in its path.

   _____

   _____

4. The earthquake caused great cracks in the earth to open.

   _____

   _____

5. The volcano emitted fumes that were harmful and deadly.

   _____

   _____

6. The point at the centre of the earthquake was the coast of Los Angeles.

   _____

   _____

7. The series of tremors after the main quake were strong enough to rattle the dishes.

   _____

   _____

8. The point at the centre of the hurricane is calm and quiet.

   _____

   _____

Exercise B

Fill in each blank in the following sentences with a word from the list below.

cyclic	factor	preparation
degradation	infrastructure	substandard
devastated	phenomenon	vulnerability
drought		

1. After the devastating hurricane, the government had to invest billions in _____ to rebuild the city.

2. _____ weather patterns help forecasters predict the weather.

3. The twister _____ the entire town.

4. Often your ability to survive a natural disaster depends on your advance _____ for such an event.

5. The severe _____ in the Prairie provinces has cost farmers millions in lost crops.

6. When determining the impact of a natural disaster, you have to _____ in the impact on the environment and people living in the area.

7. Stripping the land of fossil fuels has led to the _____ of our environment

8. The strange behaviour of animals just before major weather storms are about to hit is a _____ that scientists can't explain.

9. All the buildings that were _____ according to the current building codes were destroyed in the earthquake.

10. Our agency assesses cities to identify their _____ to natural disasters and makes recommendations to decrease potential disasters.

Vocabulary Expansion 1

Exercise C
Adjective-noun collocations

When describing the weather, certain adjectives are commonly used. Match the adjectives in Column A with the nouns in Column B. Some adjectives may be used with more than one noun. Write a sentence for each adjective-noun collocation on a separate sheet.

Column A	Column B
blinding	breeze
driving	rain
drizzling	snow
freezing	wind
gale-force	
granular	
heavy	
light	
north-easterly	
packing	
pelting	
pleasant	
pouring	
powdery	
spitting	
strong	

Exercise D

The following words describe the intensity of certain types of weather. Write the words in the lines provided above the bar line, positioning them according to their degree of intensity. Words that describe a lesser intensity should be placed at the lighter-coloured end of the bar line and words describing a greater intensity should be positioned at the darker end.

1. RAIN: downpour / mist / drizzle / spitting

   _____ _____ _____ _____

2. SNOW: packing / powdery / heavy / light / blinding

   _____ _____ _____ _____ _____

3. WIND: gale-force / strong / light / high

   _____ _____ _____ _____

Grammar Focus 1

PASSIVE VOICE
Exercise A

Change active voice to passive voice in the following sentences.

1. Scientists who study the earth's atmosphere have issued predictions of impending doom for the past few years.

   _____

   _____

2. A rise in carbon emissions has caused global warming.

   _____

   _____

3. Individual researchers made statements that human activity has contributed to global warming.

   _____

   _____

4. The world must take drastic steps to reduce the emissions of heat-trapping gases.

   _____

   _____

5. Rising oceans will flood huge tracts of densely populated land.

   _____

   _____

6. Complex computers simulate the effects of carbon dioxide emissions, methane, and chlorofluorocarbons.

   _____

   _____

Exercise B

Change passive voice to active voice in the following sentences.

1. The effects of global warming can be masked by the aerosols which cool the planet by blocking the sun.

   _____

   _____

2. Many beaches will be submerged by water from melting glaciers.

   _____

   _____

3. Temperature and rainfall patterns will be affected by global warming.

_____

_____

4. Our world climate is influenced by deep ocean currents.

_____

_____

5. Emissions must be reduced to the same levels as in the 1920s.

_____

_____

6. The lead role in reducing global warming must be taken by the industrialized nations.

_____

_____

Exercise C

Review the use of the passive voice on page 5 of your Student Book. What use does the passive voice have in the following sentences?

> ₁ Some of the harshest weather conditions in Canada are found on the island of Newfoundland. ₂ Every year, the city of St. John's is hit by fierce snowstorms that leave the inhabitants snowed in for days. ₃ Classes are cancelled and businesses are closed as the residents try to dig themselves out from Mother Nature's wrath. ₄ Often the police issue an order that states, "Only emergency vehicles and snow-clearing equipment are allowed to be on the roads" during these severe storms. ₅ Newfoundlanders are thought of as resilient individuals by most Canadians. ₆ Although Newfoundland is a beautiful island, the winter weather is regarded as a major detraction to living there.

1. _____
2. _____
3. _____
4. _____
5. _____
6. _____

Exercise D

When the passive voice is used, the performer of the action can often be omitted. The performer is included when the agent of the action is unexpected or requires identification. Circle the performing agents in the following sentences and cross them out where possible.

1. The need for increased government protection of the environment in Australia has been identified by scientists.
2. Countless articles have been written by David Suzuki condemning our treatment of the environment.
3. Native myths explaining the forces of nature have been recorded by various people.
4. The results of the greenhouse effect have been grossly miscalculated by scientists.
5. Impending changes in climate can be predicted by humans through observing animals.

Grammar in Use
Exercise E

Public notices often contain the passive voice. This impersonal structure gives a formal tone to the message. Look at the following notices and determine where each notice might be found.

1.

NO SMOKING ALLOWED.
Offenders will be fined $500.

2.

ALL EMERGENCY EXITS MUST BE KEPT CLEAR.

3.

PRIVATE PROPERTY
Trespassers will be prosecuted.

4.

Disposable diapers must not be flushed down toilets.

5.

No compensation will be paid for damage due to natural disasters or acts of war.

Vocabulary Expansion 2

Exercise A

Match the nouns in Column A with the appropriate definitions in Column B.

Column A	Column B
1. natural disaster	a) natural resource that can be replenished
2. relief agency	b) notice of impending bad weather
3. storm warning	c) an event caused by nature that has catastrophic consequences
4. global warming	d) increase in Earth's temperature and changes in climate
5. renewable resource	e) organization that provides aid to those in need

Exercise B

Nature-related idioms are common. Write definitions or explanations for the idioms underlined in the following sentences.

1. It's <u>raining cats and dogs</u> out there. Unless you have a raincoat and an umbrella, you're going to get soaked.

   _____

   _____

2. Kim spent all of Alain's money and then left him <u>high and dry</u> with a lot of bills to pay and no money.

   _____

   _____

3. Lucas did an amazing <u>snow job</u> on his mother. She actually believed him when he told her the teacher said he didn't have to attend classes on Fridays.

   _____

   _____

4. Gaitree likes to sit around and <u>shoot the breeze</u> with her co-workers at lunch in order to keep up on all the latest news.

   _____

   _____

5. Our dream of owning our own house <u>bit the dust</u> because we just couldn't make it financially feasible.

   _____

   _____

6. I want to <u>hit the hay</u> early tonight. I haven't been to bed before midnight all week.

   _____

   _____

7. Habib <u>went out on a limb</u> to start his new business. I hope that the financial risk he is taking pays off handsomely.

   _____

   _____

8. I'll <u>take a rain check</u> for that invitation. Unfortunately, I already have plans for Saturday. How about Monday?

   _____

   _____

Grammar Focus 2

PASSIVE VOICE TENSES

Exercise A

Change the following active verbs into passive voice and create a sentence using each verb. Identify the tense of the sentence.

EXAMPLE: purchased: was / were purchased

The land was purchased by an environmental protection group. = past tense

1. recorded

   _____

   _____

2. control

   _____

   _____

3. are destroying

   _____

   _____

4. were ignoring

   _____

   _____

5. have observed

   _____

   _____

6. had decided

_____

_____

7. will develop

_____

_____

Exercise B

Rewrite the following sentences by beginning each one with the words provided in parentheses.

1. A First Nations tribe from Niagara created a myth about a beautiful maiden to explain the origin of Horseshoe Falls. (A myth)

   _____

   _____

2. The sun divided the earth into several parts, separated by many great lakes. (The earth)

   _____

   _____

3. The Aboriginal people of Australia consider Ayers Rock a spiritual place. (Ayers Rock)

   _____

   _____

4. The Inuit carved blocks out of snow to build igloos. (Blocks)

   _____

   _____

5. Powerful spirits control the weather. (The weather)

   _____

   _____

Exercise C

Choose whether to use the active or passive form of the verbs in parentheses and then write your choice in the blanks provided.

David Suzuki ₁ _____ (be) a champion of environmental protection. He supports the notion that environmental education must ₂ _____ (teach) from cradle to grave and must ₃ _____ (become) part of a required curriculum for engineers, agriculturalists, teachers, lawyers, and anyone else who ₄ _____ (make) decisions affecting the environment. The knowledge must ₅ _____ (be) current and ongoing programs must ₆ _____ (develop and

study). People must ₇ _____ (unlearn) the bad habits of consumption and exploitation practised by our ancestors. Individual responsibility must ₈ _____ (take). It's imperative that we understand nature and that it become part of our hearts and souls. Long-term rather than short-term strategies must ₉ _____ (embrace).

Grammar in Use

Exercise D

The following tips on reducing your carbon footprint have been written in a very impersonal style using several passive structures. There are many things that we can do as individuals to decrease our impact on the environment. In order to persuade people to reduce their carbon footprints, rewrite the tips in a less impersonal tone, using the active voice where possible.

Six things to be done to reduce your carbon footprint

1. Ensure that all materials that are recyclable have been separated from non-recyclable materials when you put out your garbage.

   Separate all recyclables from your garbage.

2. Lights should be turned off if you are not in the room.

   _____

3. Compact fluorescent bulbs should be used instead of energy-wasting incandescent bulbs.

   _____

4. All electronics must be unplugged when you are not using them.

   _____

5. Cars emit harmful exhaust and use precious natural resources. Public transportation should be used.

   _____

6. Old appliances in your home should be replaced with new energy-efficient models.

   _____

Grammar Expansion

In informal or spoken English, *get* can substitute for *be* as the auxiliary verb in the passive voice.

EXAMPLE: Jolene **was selected** because of her knowledge of volcanoes.

Jolene **got selected** because of her knowledge of volcanoes.

Get is used in the passive voice in informal situations when:

- the process is being emphasized.
  The garbage gets picked up twice a week.

- the subject is animate.
  David Suzuki got fired for his opinions.

- the situation is bad.
  Over one hundred people got killed in that quake.

Exercise E

Complete the following sentences using appropriate forms of the verbs *to be* or *to get*. In some cases both may be appropriate. Explain your choices.

1. Environmental pollution _____ blamed for many birth defects.

2. David Suzuki _____ recognized wherever he goes.

3. A fox _____ hurt by the steel trap.

4. A machine _____ built to study the impact of carbon emissions on the atmosphere.

5. Jason _____ hit by a bolt of lightning.

Note: The verb *be* is always possible, but *get* is only possible in informal situations.

One Step Beyond—Create an Activity
Exercise F

Create ten sentences in the passive voice that describe the location, origin, or purpose of various things. Write these sentences on a piece of paper, leaving a blank line for the subject item. Exchange your exercise with a classmate and try to identify the missing things.

EXAMPLE: _____ was invented by Alexander Graham Bell.

The telephone was invented by Alexander Graham Bell.

Exercise G

Write a paragraph for potential visitors to your native country, warning them about one type of severe weather condition that frequently occurs. Describe the weather condition and what should be done if it occurs. Use both passive and active voices, as well as vocabulary from the unit. Then rewrite the paragraph as a fill-in-the-blank activity. Replace each verb with a blank followed by the base form of the verb in brackets [ ]. Also replace all the weather-related words with blanks, followed by the word scrambled and in parentheses ( ). Exchange your exercise with a partner.

EXAMPLE: In Southwestern Ontario, _____ (nneful) clouds race across the land destroying everything in their path. Life-saving steps must _____ [take] if you see a _____ (ntoarod).

Writing

Prewriting

Prewriting is an essential part of the writing process; it allows you to get your ideas down so that you can look at them. Often, the most difficult aspect of writing is getting started. There are several prewriting steps that writers should routinely follow in order to produce better pieces of writing.

The Topic

One stumbling block facing many writers is how to get started when presented with a topic. You may not know how to narrow down the topic or how much you really know about that topic. In order to get the "creative juices flowing," it is essential to spend five to ten minutes doing a prewriting activity.

Brainstorming

The following are three ways to generate ideas using brainstorming. The purpose of brainstorming is to generate an excess of ideas. From these ideas, you select the ones that help you focus on your topic, and discard those that do not support your topic. It is not necessary to use all three methods; after experimenting with each, you will find the one that works best for you.

1. Freewriting

For ten minutes, write as many ideas as you can think of about a topic. *Don't worry about spelling, grammar, or punctuation.* The purpose is to record free thoughts that you will sort out at a later point.

EXAMPLE: Topic—Devastating Floods

Manitoba witnessed some of the most devastating floods ever witnessed in that province. Millions of doolars in damages volunteers from all over came to help out. Many people donated clothes, blankets and non-perishable food items to help out the flood victims — the red Cross was overwelmed wioth the donations. Many people couldn't return to their homes for several weeks and had no idea how damafged their homes would be when they returned. Animals and pets were sometimes left sttranded in the fast exedus — volunteers in boats captured animals and attempted to reunite with their owners. Military played a key role...

2. Cluster Map

Draw a circle in the middle of the page and write the name of your topic inside the circle. Then draw six to eight lines radiating from the circle like the spokes of a wheel. At the end of each line, draw another circle. Write words or phrases that relate to the topic in these secondary circles. From the secondary circles, draw radiating lines to another set of circles. Fill these new circles with words or phrases related to the words or phrases in each secondary circle.

EXAMPLE:

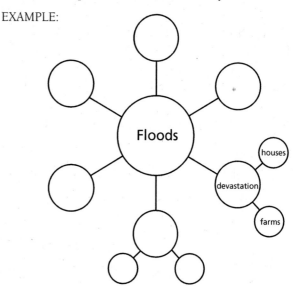

3. Star Map

Draw a six-pointed star and write the name of your topic inside the star. Label the points of the star with the question words: Who? What? When? Where? Why? How? Consider the answers to each question as they relate to the topic and jot down this information beside each point of the star. (These are also known as the reporters' questions or W5H questions.)

EXAMPLE:

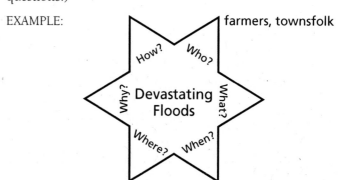

Who?   farmers, townsfolk, military, volunteers
What? flood relief, evacuation, tragedy, loss
When? spring
Where? Manitoba, Minnesota
Why?   rain, melting snow, high water levels, broken dams
How?   act of nature, human struggles

Identify the Audience

It is very important to think about your audience before you start the writing process. Language and content will be influenced by the assumptions you make about the intended reader.

Narrowing the Topic

The topic you choose has to be sufficiently narrowed in order to be adequately developed in whatever length of paragraph or essay you are required to write. If you were asked to write on the topic of **floods**, you could easily write about several aspects of floods such as recent floods, great historical floods, deaths due to floods, or the tremendous costs of floods. If you were asked to write only a paragraph, however, you would have to narrow the topic to encompass only one aspect of floods—for example, **spring floods in Manitoba**. This could still be too large a topic to deal with as the floods in Manitoba could encompass many aspects—for example, economic costs, the ruin of farmland, and the role of the army in relief efforts. Once you have selected one aspect of the topic, you can write your topic sentence.

The Topic Sentence

The topic sentence states the main idea of the paragraph; all other sentences in the paragraph must relate to the topic sentence. It is usually general in content in order to introduce all the ideas that follow. It must also express a controlling idea that indicates the writer's attitude towards the topic. It is usually the first sentence of the paragraph because it tells what the paragraph is about, but can also be positioned as the second or concluding sentence.

Exercise A

The following sentences are possible topic sentences for a paragraph about the spring floods in Manitoba. Underline the controlling idea in each sentence.

1. The economic damage caused by the floods in Manitoba is still being calculated.
2. Farmers lost a lifetime of work as the Manitoba floods washed away their livelihood.
3. The army played a key role in the aftermath of the floods.
4. Volunteers came to help the flood victims in any way they could.

Note: Because the topic sentence is key to writing an effective paragraph, it should be a complete sentence (containing a subject and verb and expressing a complete thought) and be limited in scope.

Exercise B

Place a checkmark beside the sentences below that make effective topic sentences.

- [ ] 1. We don't care about our environment.
- [ ] 2. Global warming poses a serious threat to our weather.
- [ ] 3. Global warming is a big problem.
- [ ] 4. Which means cars are major polluters.
- [ ] 5. The future of our planet is in our hands.
- [ ] 6. The environment.

Exercise C

In the following paragraphs, underline the topic sentence that states the main idea of each paragraph.

1. Our lives are greatly influenced by the weather; it affects how we dress, how we feel, and what we do daily. As we step out of our front doors each day, we are subjected to nature's whims. Before venturing outdoors, we check the weather to ensure that we are dressed appropriately. A light jacket would offer no protection against the bitter cold winds in early winter, for example. In addition to influencing our choice of clothing, the weather also affects us physically. Many people suffering from physical ailments, such as arthritis, feel the discomfort of impending rain as it makes their joints ache. This may limit the activities they are able to partake in on those wet, rainy days. Physical discomfort is not the only way in which weather affects our daily activities. No one in his or her right mind would start out on a long drive during blizzard conditions. When the sun blazes and it becomes unbearably hot, we may be prisoners in our air-conditioned homes. The weather definitely influences our daily lives through how we dress, our state of health, and the activities we partake in.

2. First Nations peoples peacefully co-exist with nature. They believe that they should not take more from the land than they can use. When they fish and hunt, it is to feed themselves, not for commercial exploitation. Moreover, they show their respect for the land by thanking the spirits for its use. The First Nations peoples' treatment of the land will ensure that it is still fruitful for future generations. Some other cultures have tried to conquer nature. Not content to take just

enough from the land for their own sustenance, they seek to make a commercial profit from it. The aim is to conquer, not co-exist. The result is a dying planet. The First Nations peoples have learned to live in harmony with nature, but many other cultures have not.

Exercise D

Write topic sentences for the following topics. Remember that the topic sentences must have a controlling idea and be limited in scope to ensure a coherent paragraph. Brainstorm your topic using the prewriting techniques previously outlined.

1. The environment

_____

_____

2. Native myths

_____

_____

3. Famous scientists

_____

_____

4. The origin of the planet

_____

_____

5. Nature's power

_____

_____

6. Natural disasters

_____

_____

☑ **Prewriting Checklist**

☐ Did I brainstorm ideas?

☐ Did I clearly identify the audience?

☐ Is my topic sufficiently narrowed?

☐ Is my topic sentence a complete sentence expressing a complete thought?

☐ Does my topic sentence introduce the topic?

☐ Does my topic sentence contain a controlling idea?

Academic Word List

adequate	elements	potential
affect	estimate	proportions
area	factors	region
community	funds	rejected
complex	generated	research
consequences	issues	variable
cycle	major	

Exercise A

Word Meaning

Circle the word that best matches the meaning.

1. component or part (research / region / element)
2. circumstances which influence the result (factors / elements / areas)
3. dimensions or size (major / proportions / funds)
4. a group of people living in a specific area (factors / issues / community)
5. systematic study to establish facts (estimate / research / issues)
6. sufficient for the purpose (adequate / complex / variable)
7. able to be changed (affect / generate / variable)
8. complicated or intricate (complex / proportions / consequences)
9. refuse to consider or agree to (estimate / reject / generate)
10. financial resources (community / areas / funds)
11. to make a difference to (affect / research / generate)
12. important, serious, significant (adequate / major / variable)
13. to approximate (estimate / research / generate)
14. results of effects (proportions / issues / consequences)
15. to produce (generate / research / reject)
16. a certain area or part (cycle / region / element)
17. a geographical region (area / element / cycle)
18. the possibility of something happening (cyclical / potential / complex)
19. something that is regularly repeated (funds / proportions / cycle)
20. important topics for consideration (issues / research / region)

Exercise B

Listen to your teacher or an audio dictionary to hear the pronunciation for each word in the list. Repeat each word aloud. Mark the syllables and major word stress.

EXAMPLE: adequate (adj): **ǎd** / e / quate

1. affect (v): _____
2. area (n): _____
3. community (n): _____
4. complex (adj): _____
5. consequences (n): _____
6. cycle (n): _____
7. elements (n): _____
8. estimate (v): _____
9. factors (n): _____
10. funds (n): _____
11. generated (v): _____
12. issues (n): _____
13. major (adj): _____
14. potential (n): _____
15. proportions (n): _____
16. region (n): _____
17. rejected (v): _____
18. research (n): _____
19. variable (adj): _____

Exercise C

Word Forms

Fill in the blanks with the word form indicated in parentheses. More than one word may be possible for the indicated word form.

1. adequate (adj): _____ (adv)
2. affect (v): _____ (adj)
   _____ (adv)
3. complex (adj): _____ (n)
4. consequences (n): _____ (adj)
   _____ (adv)
5. cycle (n): _____ (adj)
6. elements (n): _____ (adj)
7. estimate (v): _____ (n)
   _____ (adj)
8. factors (n): _____ (v)
9. funds (n): _____ (n)

10. generated (v): _____ (n)
11. major (adj): _____ (n)
12. potential (n): _____ (adj)
    _____ (adv)
13. proportions (n): _____ (adj)
    _____ (adv)
14. region (n): _____ (adj)
    _____ (adv)
15. rejected (v): _____ (n)
16. research (n): _____ (n)
17. variable (adj): _____ (n)
    _____ (v)

Exercise D

In a dictionary, find one example sentence for each circled word in Exercise A and copy it into your notebook. Draft a second sentence of your own. Then, work with a partner to revise and edit your sentence.

Exercise E

Read the following story and complete each blank with one of the words from the list. You do not have to change the grammatical form of any of the words. Use each word only once.

adequately	consequently	major
affected	cyclical	potential
areas	factors	researchers
communities		

No matter where in the world you live, you have to ₁ _____ prepare to survive a natural disaster. Disasters such as hurricanes are ₂ _____ and can be predicted. People in ₃ _____ that are ₄ _____ by hurricanes know the ₅ _____ destruction that a hurricane can cause. Whole ₆ _____ that live along the coastline have been utterly destroyed by the gale-force winds and ₇ _____ many lives have been lost. ₈ _____ continue to track these storms in an attempt to identify ₉ _____ that will indicate the severity of ₁₀ _____ hurricanes in advance so lives can be saved.

complex	funding	reject
disproportionate	generate	variable
elements	issues	
estimate	regions	

Predicting severe weather is a ₁₁ _____ endeavour. Experts attempt to ₁₂ _____ just how nature's

13 _____ 14 _____ will behave. Some 15 _____ receive a 16 _____ number of hurricanes and earthquakes compared to other areas of the world. This raises 17 _____ related to the 18 _____ of disaster relief efforts. Wealthy countries that don't experience many devastating disasters should be expected to 19 _____ aid to poor countries. Some wealthy countries 20 _____ this responsibility.

Unit 2
Strange But True

Vocabulary

Exercise A

Complete the following paragraph by filling in the blanks with appropriate words from the vocabulary list below.

astrology	psychic	subconscious
clairvoyance	reincarnation	telepathy
numerology		

Belief in $_1$ _____ phenomena is common throughout the world. Canadians are not the only ones, for example, who enjoy reading their horoscopes daily in the newspapers; many cultures believe in $_2$ _____. The idea that the stars influence personalities and human behaviour in some way has existed for centuries. In fact, some cultures even believe in $_3$ _____—the idea that numbers influence our luck. Incidents of $_4$ _____ and $_5$ _____ are frequently reported in the media. In one case, a father saved the life of his daughter, who had fallen into a flooding river on the way home from school, because he could "see in his mind" that his daughter was in danger. In another case, a woman in Halifax claimed she could communicate in thought with her sister in Ontario. The sisters appeared to have the ability to read each other's minds so that one sister could actually "tell" the other that she had fallen down a flight of stairs. Some argue that such incidents are simply physical cues planted in the $_6$ _____ mind. In other words, we read cues from the physical world and store them in our minds without being aware of them consciously. $_7$ _____ is perhaps one of the most commonly held beliefs. The very notion that our existence ceases at death is very difficult to comprehend. Not only do some people believe in a life "somewhere else" after our earthly death, many believe that we actually come back to earth as a new life form—a person, an animal, or even a plant. Unfortunately, it is very difficult to confirm the existence of paranormal events scientifically. That is why, despite our belief in the supernatural, it remains just that—a belief, not a fact.

Exercise B

Complete the crossword by filling in the blanks using the words below.

apparitions	omens	seance
curse	poltergeist	shaman
levitate	premonitions	telepathy
medium	psychokinetic	voodoo

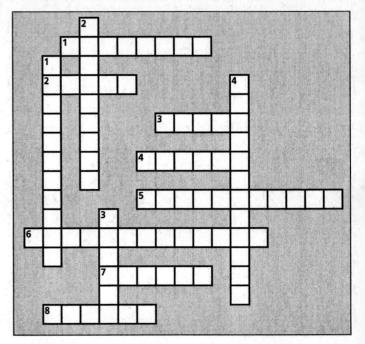

Across

1. A Polish medium named Stanislawa Tomczyk could _____ small objects between her hands, such as small balls and cigarettes. It looked as if she was controlling them by threads as if they were puppets. On one occasion, a teaspoon threw itself out of a glass after she had concentrated on it.

2. The Romans were very superstitious. When making decisions, many emperors had personal astrologers who advised them. There were also priests and priestesses who interpreted _____ from the gods.

3. A 12th-century writer called Giraldus Cambrensis wrote about a _____ put upon the inhabitants of the region of Ossary in Ireland in the 6th century. Every seven years, two people from the region had to become wolves. If they survived, they were allowed to return to their old lives, and two more people had to take their places.

12

4. A major religion of Haiti, _____, is centred around ceremonies in which the worshippers are taken possession of by spirits.

5. Those who practise spirit religions often claim to be able to summon up _____ of demons, spirits, and even animals. One witness to an African ceremony described how he saw a young girl dance a "leopard dance" by firelight. As she danced, the witness could see shadows all around her which his companion said were clearly leopards. At the high point of the dance, three real leopards suddenly appeared, walked across the clearing, and disappeared back into the jungle. It was as if they had come to investigate the phantom leopards called up by the dance.

6. In 1983, Carole Compton, a nanny in Italy, was brought to court and accused of deliberately starting fires in the homes where she worked. During the trial, however, it emerged that the fires behaved oddly—one did not burn the spot where it started, for instance, although surrounding furniture was charred. It was believed by many that Carole had unconscious _____ ability to start fires.

7. While trying to contact the dead, the _____ goes into a trance and the spirits may show their presence by moving objects, such as a table.

8. In a typical _____, people sit in a circle and touch hands to help concentration (and to make sure that no one cheats!).

Down

1. Was a _____ responsible for moving the coffins in a sealed family vault in Barbados? Between 1812 and 1820, every time the vault was opened to bring in another coffin, the place was found in disarray. The coffins lay at all angles, and sometimes stood upright as if they had been flung across the chamber.

2. _____ is difficult to control as it needs the participation of two or more people—one actively trying to transmit his or her thoughts, and the other trying to receive and understand them.

3. A tribal _____ has to go through rigorous initiation rites before beginning practice.

4. Sometimes accidents are avoided through _____. One man, while on holiday in Scotland, sent his daughter out for a walk. Suddenly, he "knew" that she was in danger, and sent a servant who found her going to the beach to sit on some stones by a railway bridge. Later, they heard that an engine fell off the bridge and onto the stones at the time she would have been there.

One Step Beyond—Create an Activity
Exercise C

Write a short paragraph in pencil about the supernatural, using at least three of the words from Exercises A and B. Erase the three vocabulary words and exchange your paper with a classmate. Can your classmate fill in the blanks with the correct words?

Vocabulary Expansion

Exercise A

Read the following sentences to determine the meanings of the prefixes. Write the meanings of the words and the prefixes.

1. a) During hypnosis, the patient was instructed that she would no longer believe in ghosts when she awoke. As a result of this posthypnotic suggestion, the patient was cured of her fear of ghosts.
   b) The work of many great artists, including Vincent Van Gogh, was not recognized during their lifetimes, but rather posthumously.
   posthypnotic _____
   posthumously _____
   post- _____

2. a) Scientists have attempted to provide scientific explanations for many paranormal occurrences in an effort to demystify the supernatural.
   b) Classifying shamans as magicians demeans their role as healers and spiritual leaders.
   demystify _____
   demean _____
   de- _____

3. a) In an out-of-body experience, the body transcends the physical world.
   b) Spirits sometimes use mediums to transmit messages to others.
   transcend _____
   transmit _____
   trans- _____

4. a) Monotheistic religions believe in only one god; there are other religions, however, that believe in several gods.
   b) The belief in the supernatural may be just an interesting pursuit in an otherwise monotonous existence.
   monotheistic _____
   monotonous _____
   mono- _____

5. a) The woman was <u>dis</u>satisfied with the explanation that her premonition about the plane crash was coincidental.
   b) The television psychic was <u>dis</u>credited when it was revealed that 90 percent of his predictions failed to come true.
   dissatisfied _____
   discredited _____
   dis- _____

6. a) A curse is also known as a <u>mal</u>ediction because when someone puts a curse on you that person speaks a word or sentence asking for something bad to happen to you.
   b) Not all ghosts are <u>mal</u>icious; some are well-meaning and pleasant.
   malediction _____
   malicious _____
   mal- _____

Exercise B

Some prefixes have more than one meaning. Using the meanings given in the answer key for Exercise A, brainstorm as many words as you can for each prefix. Then choose two words from the list for each prefix and create two sentences using these words.

Exercise C
Wordbuilding

Use the prefixes presented in this unit (Student Book and Workbook) to build words. Attach appropriate prefixes to the words below. Use a dictionary to confirm that the words you choose are appropriate. Write them on a separate sheet.

Prefixes			
de-	*dis-*	*mal-*	*mono-*
para-	*post-*	*pre-*	*re-*
sub-	*super-*	*tele-*	*trans-*

Words		
adjusted	agree	arrange
caffeinated	code	figure
formed	gram	heading
honest	human	marketing
mature	mission	nova
phrase	plant	port
psychology	reputable	script
secondary	view	

REPORTED SPEECH (STATEMENTS)
Exercise A

Report what these politicians said.

1. Ms. H: A few ghosts from my past have come back to haunt me.
   Ms. H. admitted _____
   _____

2. Mr. B: There were many unexplained events in this government last year.
   Mr. B. said _____
   _____

3. Mr. J: I believe that the leader was a fox in his previous life.
   Mr. J. was overheard saying _____
   _____

4. Mr. M: I predict that my party will balance the budget this year.
   Mr. M. predicted _____
   _____

5. Mr. P: I am learning to speak a second language because I have discovered that being monolingual in a bilingual country is a curse.
   Mr. P. assured voters _____
   _____

6. Mr. J: I envision a country my children and grandchildren can be proud of.
   Mr. J. announced _____
   _____

7. Mr. L: One doesn't have to be a psychic to know that governing a bilingual country will continue to be a challenge in the future.
   Mr. L. said _____
   _____

Exercise B

Identify the reported speech in this news report from the weekly tabloid, *Star Gazing*, and quote what the speakers must have said.

Yesterday the Academy of Space Science announced that a possible UFO had been sighted by one of its senior research scientists at its California observatory. Jerome Harrold, Executive Director of the Academy, said that Dr. Marilyn Boch had reported seeing a spaceship-like object at about 10:15 p.m. on Tuesday night. Dr. Boch immediately began to take pictures of the unusual object with one of the observatory's telescopic cameras. Mr. Harrold admitted that he was sceptical about the sighting, despite the photographs. When interviewed later, Dr. Boch confirmed that she had been working in the Academy's observatory when she saw a gold, oval-shaped flying machine racing through the night sky. According to Dr. Boch, sightings of this nature are quite common but rarely reported.

The senior scientist acknowledged that other scientists had also seen UFOs but had not reported them because they didn't want to jeopardize their reputations. She admitted that the government was putting pressure on the scientific community to withhold information about UFO sightings in order to avoid mass panic.

Harrold denied this and suggested that perhaps Dr. Boch had been watching too many episodes of *Unsolved Mysteries*. He assured *Star Gazing* that the Academy would hold a complete investigation into the sighting.

What did these individuals say to the reporter?

Jerome Harrold: _____
_____

Jerome Harrold: _____
_____

Jerome Harrold: _____
_____

Jerome Harrold: _____
_____

Dr. Marilyn Boch: _____
_____

Dr. Marilyn Boch: _____
_____

Dr. Marilyn Boch: _____
_____

Dr. Marilyn Boch: _____
_____

REPORTED SPEECH (QUESTIONS)
Exercise A
A reported interview

A psychology graduate student interviewed Noel about his beliefs and experiences with the paranormal. Based on Noel's reported answers, create the questions the interviewer might have asked.

EXAMPLE: *Reported response*: Noel said he did believe in the supernatural.

Reported question: The interviewer asked Noel if he believed in the supernatural.

1. Noel said he read his horoscope about once a week.
   The interviewer asked Noel _____
   _____
   _____

2. Noel replied that he had had paranormal experiences.
   The interviewer asked Noel _____
   _____
   _____

3. Noel said he had experienced about ten supernatural phenomena in his life.
   The interviewer asked Noel _____
   _____
   _____

4. Noel answered that he didn't know what "psychokinesis" was.
   The interviewer asked Noel _____
   _____
   _____

5. Noel said that his most recent paranormal experience happened about a year ago.
   The interviewer asked Noel _____
   _____
   _____

6. Noel stated that he doesn't think he is psychic.
   The interviewer asked Noel _____
   _____
   _____

7. Noel said that he would consider participating in an experiment involving levitation.

The interviewer asked Noel _____

_____

_____

8. Noel agreed that he would call the interviewer's office to confirm the time of the experiment.

The interviewer asked Noel _____

_____

_____

Grammar in Use

Exercise B

Reported Speech (Statements and Questions)

Read "A Cradle of Love," which is a true account of an experience with the supernatural, and then answer the following questions using reported speech.

1. What did the boy on the terrace shout to Daniel as he arrived for the party?

_____

_____

2. What did Daniel's friends ask him after he had fallen through the skylight?

_____

_____

3. What did José's mother tell Daniel as she hugged him?

_____

_____

4. What did José's father say about Daniel's "lucky" fall?

_____

_____

5. What did Daniel conclude about how the old chair had got there?

_____

_____

A Cradle of Love

Eight-year-old Daniel lived in Buenos Aires, a huge city in Argentina, South America. Here, the architecture is very mixed, with high apartment buildings like towers next to two-story buildings, and low houses all around. Today was the day Daniel was going to attend his friend José's birthday party. He was very excited for children here, as everywhere, love parties!

José lived just two blocks away from Daniel. The two always walked to school together, and Daniel had often played on the big terrace in the back of José's house. From the terrace, the boys could see the roofs of surrounding houses. A wall separated them from the building next door.

That afternoon, Daniel walked to José's house, carrying a birthday present for him. Several boys were already on the terrace. "Hey, Daniel!" one shouted. "You're just in time to play ball."

Daniel joined his pals, and the boys threw the ball around. All of a sudden someone missed a catch, and the ball sailed over the wall onto the roof of the building next door. Instantly, the boys climbed up the wall and scrambled onto the roof.

"There's the ball!" Daniel saw it first, lying on top of a glass skylight. Daniel had seen such skylights before, on top of his school's roof. Skylights save energy by letting

sun inside, and Daniel knew the glass they used was very hard. This large pane would hold an eight-year-old boy easily. Daniel stepped up onto the skylight, reached for the ball, and...

Crash! The window shattered into a million pieces. Daniel fell through it, and hurtled toward the basement floor below.

16

His fall seemed to take hours. Feeling as if he were in slow motion, Daniel spun upside down and around, completely out of control. Finally, he landed.

But…although he had fallen more than two stories, he seemed to be fine. Gingerly, Daniel felt his head, arms, and legs. Nothing was broken. He sat up. In spite of all the jagged glass surrounding him, he could see only one small cut on his right arm. It didn't even hurt. Nothing hurt.

"Daniel? Are you all right?" His friends were shouting down from the top of the roof near the skylight.

"I think so," he called back. He slowly got to his feet, grateful but confused. Soon he heard a key turn in a door and José's parents came running in to find him.

José's mother gave him a big hug. "The people who live in this house are on vacation," she explained. "They left their key with us."

José's father was looking around. "Daniel must have landed on this chair," he said. "That's what broke his fall."

Daniel turned around. There was an old ugly armchair behind him, tilting because of a broken leg. He had landed on it before hitting the floor; now he remembered.

But something was very odd. Daniel realized he was in a luxurious living room, beautifully furnished. Why would such an old chair be in a room like this? Especially right underneath a skylight—as if it had been placed there just for him?

No one, not even the owners of the house, ever discovered who owned the chair, or where it had come from. "I thought it was a great coincidence at first," Daniel says. "But now I believe my guardian angel moved that chair from somewhere else, to save my life. He was watching out for me that day. And he still does."

Exercise C

You overheard the following conversation yesterday evening at a restaurant. Report the conversation to a friend.

Jost: Hi. How did your day go?

Sandy: You wouldn't believe what happened to me today. I had the most bizarre experience. I mean, it was freaky.

Jost: You're kidding! What happened?

Sandy: After I took the kids to school this morning, I was driving along Main Street and when I stopped at the traffic light, I saw a ghost. I mean, I saw this apparition… this ghost-like figure heading towards my car. I couldn't tell if it was a man or a woman, but it seemed to be a young person.

Jost: Are you serious? Come on Sandy, you're putting me on—right?

Sandy: I'm not kidding you. I know it sounds crazy, but it's true. This "thing" came towards my car and I opened the side window.

Jost: You did what? Weren't you afraid? Why didn't you run it over?

Sandy: Run over a ghost, Jost? Besides, I wasn't afraid.

Jost: This is just too bizarre. I don't believe you.

Sandy: It gets better. So I rolled down my window and it says, "Help me! Help me! I'm dying!" At this point I thought I was going crazy, but I wasn't afraid. And then all of a sudden it disappeared. As the light changed, I drove on and just at the next corner I turned my head for some reason and I saw that there was some construction on one of the side streets. For some inexplicable reason, I felt drawn to the site. I just had this sense that I needed to pull over and check it out. The work crew wasn't there. There was a large hole in the ground that had been covered with boards, but a few of the boards were broken. I looked down and even though it was dark, I could see a body. It wasn't moving. The person was clearly unconscious.

Jost: Did you report this to the police?

Sandy: Of course. I ran to my cell phone and called the police immediately. An ambulance came and got the teen out. When I saw him, I recognized him as the apparition that had approached my car. They pronounced him dead on the scene and took him to the hospital. I told them what had happened to me and of course they didn't believe me. But I followed them to the hospital and half an hour later they told me he was alive, but in critical condition. Jost, he had come back to life! I know that this teen asked me to save his life, and I did.

Jost: You must be psychic or something.

Now report the conversation, using the following lines as your introduction:

Last night at a restaurant, I heard a woman telling her husband about a paranormal experience she had had. Her husband asked her _____

_____

_____

_____

_____

_____

_____

_____

_____

_____

_____

_____

Grammar Expansion

Commands / Requests / Advice

In reported speech, commands are usually expressed by a command verb such as *tell*, *order*, and *command*. When expressing commands using these verbs, an object + infinitive must be used after the reporting verb.

EXAMPLE: *Quoted*: He said, "Leave me alone!"

   Reported: He told <u>me</u> <u>to leave</u> him alone.

   (object + infinitive)

When reporting a negative command, use object + *not* + infinitive.

EXAMPLE: *Quoted*: The medium announced (to the participants), "Don't delay."

   Reported: The medium advised <u>the listeners</u> <u>not</u> <u>to delay</u>.

   (object + *not* + infinitive)

Common Reporting Commands

advise	forbid	remind
command	order	urge
encourage	recommend	warn

Exercise D

Convert the quoted speech to reported speech and the reported speech to quoted speech.

1. "Stop this nonsense!" the father shouted to his son.

   _____

   _____

2. The shaman told him not to be afraid.

   _____

   _____

3. The clairvoyant told him to be careful.

   _____

   _____

4. "Get the camera!" she ordered her husband.

   _____

   _____

5. "Beware of a man with a blond beard," the medium warned the listeners.

   _____

   _____

One Step Beyond—Create an Activity
Exercise E

1. Use your imagination to write a dialogue between yourself and a friend who has just had a paranormal experience. Limit your writing to six exchanges each. Then exchange your dialogue with a partner and write your partner's dialogue in reported speech. Finally, work with your partner to edit each of your reported accounts.

2. Imagine that you have encountered one of the following supernatural figures: a fairy, a vampire, a witch, or an apparition. Complete a police report. Report the details of the encounter and a detailed description of the figure. Exchange reports with a partner (police artist), who will use it to sketch the figure.

Writing

The Narrative Paragraph

The narrative paragraph tells a story which explains something. You may want to explain a strange but true experience that happened to you. In this case, you would include important details such as who was involved; what happened; and where, when, why, and how it happened.

An effective narrative paragraph

- has a clear purpose (it makes a point).
- includes only those aspects and details that are relevant to your point.
- is arranged in chronological order.
- uses transitions to signal relationships, especially time relationships.
- uses precise words to paint a written picture of the story.

Common narratives that most people are familiar with are the bedtime stories that are read to children. Soap operas are another form of the narrative.

Exercise A

The sentences below were reported by someone who had a paranormal experience. They are not in the correct order. Reconstruct the narrative paragraph by putting the sentences in the correct sequence. Indicate the sequence by numbering the sentences in the answer boxes provided.

☐ After trying to contact my great-grandfather for about 45 minutes, we were about to give up when all of a sudden the table moved. It levitated about ten centimetres above the ground. I was astonished.

☐ It was on a Sunday evening and we were sitting around the kitchen table in the dark, holding hands.

☐ I had attended the seance because I wanted to disprove my aunt's claims.

☐ Until that day, I had never had a supernatural experience and was very sceptical. Not only did my great-grandfather levitate the table, he also spoke to us through my aunt, and eventually presented himself.

☐ It was three years ago, and I was attending a seance conducted by my aunt.

☐ I was told that my aunt had acute psychic powers, and had been a medium for my paternal great-grandfather for many years.

☐ Through these encounters, I have come to understand that there is much more to the world than meets the eye.

☐ My two sisters, my mother, and my uncle were also present.

☐ I vividly recall my first encounter with the ghost of my great-grandfather.

☐ Since that first encounter, my great-grandfather's ghost has presented itself to me many times, giving me useful advice and comforting me when I needed comfort.

Exercise B

Imagine you are Daniel in the story "A Cradle of Love." Write a narrative paragraph describing what happened to you when you were eight years old. Use the Narrative Paragraph Checklist to edit your work.

Exercise C

Tell the story illustrated on the previous page in a narrative paragraph. Use the Narrative Paragraph Checklist that appears below Exercise E to edit your work. Write your story using one of the following openers.

a) I once attended a seance...

b) Last month my aunt was conducting a seance at her house...

c) My spouse and I went to a seance last week...

d) I love being a ghost...

Exercise D

There are eight grammatical errors in the paragraph below. Find the errors and then write the corrections above the lines where they appear.

What I remember most about my arrival in this country was a feeling of hope. We arrived early one ice-cold winter morning in February. My mother and father were very exhausted, having travelled for so long with four young children. I was ten. When we stepped off the plane and looked around us at the grey, icy terminal buildings, my father said that he is not sure he will be able to live here. My mother took his hand and told him not to judge a whole country on its international airport. Still, my father insisted he can feel heaviness in her bones. "We would struggle here," he said. We children were very excited despite our lack of sleep, and sadness at having left behind friends and relations. But on the walk from the plane to the terminal I felt a deep, cold chill creeping through my thin sweater. I began to feel tired, very tired, and at that moment I cursed under my breath that perhaps my father will be right. Perhaps we had made a mistake. My mother must have guessed my thoughts for she hugged me warmly and, looking into my innocent eyes, soothed me, saying that our arrival has been a blessing. With tears in my eyes, I looked up at her face. As I glanced beyond her shoulders, a faint but steady ray of sunshine was creeping through a crack in the thick winter clouds. It felt warm and soothing. I recognized it as an omen, and, as the weak sun bathed my face, I knew that she was right. Our arrival would be a blessing. Taking my father's hand, I walked towards the terminal building with a sense of renewed hope.

Exercise E

Write a narrative paragraph about your arrival in a new country. Use the Narrative Paragraph Checklist below to edit your work.

☑ **Narrative Paragraph Checklist**

☐ Have I considered my audience and my purpose?

☐ Have I narrowed my topic?

☐ Did I brainstorm to generate ideas?

☐ Does my topic sentence tell the main point of my story?

☐ Have I chosen only the important events that relate to the main point of my topic sentence?

☐ Have I chosen details that clearly relate to my main point?

☐ Do the events in my paragraph follow a chronological order?

☐ Have I used transitional expressions to show the time order?

☐ Have I checked my paragraph to make sure that the meaning of each sentence is clear?

☐ Have I checked my paragraph to make sure that I have used precise words and the correct form of words?

☐ Have I proofread my paragraph for errors in grammar, punctuation, and spelling?

Academic Word List*

approach	function	mental
challenge	indicate	perceived
conclusion	investigation	predicted
dimensions	involved	project
energy	items	reliance
exposure	job	stability
final	labour	

*includes words found in Student Book listening recordings

Exercise A

Word meaning

Choose the correct meaning of the underlined word in each sentence.

1. As the apparition slowly approached the young boy, the boy fainted.
   a) moved towards
   b) moved away
   c) moved aside

2. The woman thought her radio speakers were not functioning properly because when she turned off the radio, strange sounds continued to come from the speakers.
   a) broken
   b) working
   c) turned off

3. The fact that no one has ever been able to scientifically prove the existence of paranormal experiences indicates these experiences are illusions.
   a) is absolute proof that
   b) disproves that
   c) suggests or signals that

4. Some neuroscientists claim that the feeling of having an out-of-body experience involves an area of the brain called the angular gyrus. In other words, out-of-body experiences are tricks of the brain.
   a) includes
   b) ignores
   c) damages

5. After labouring all day in the hot sun picking grapes, Egbert packed up his belongings and turned to leave the fields. That's when he saw the ghost of his great-grandfather walking along the road.
   a) dreaming
   b) working
   c) eating

6. After many unexplained instances of strange noises, doors opening and closing by themselves, and lights turning on and off, Alisha concluded that her house was inhabited by a ghost.
   a) rejected
   b) reasoned
   c) ended

7. We tried for more than an hour to contact our deceased mother at the seance. Finally she gave us a signal that she was in the room.
   a) at last
   b) certainly
   c) consequently

8. I grew up in a house with a poltergeist who was fond of flinging small items through the air whenever my parents were entertaining guests.
   a) birds
   b) ghosts
   c) objects

9. Felix first thought his perception was distorted when he saw the apparition of his dead cat.
   a) view
   b) glasses
   c) attention

10. We should rely on reasoning as well as our senses to explain strange experiences.
    a) reject
    b) depend
    c) argue

11. The young soldier even remembered the dimensions of the room in his dreams.
    a) design
    b) size
    c) furniture

12. Neuroscientists investigate the neurological basis of out-of-body experiences.
    a) carefully study
    b) disbelieve
    c) accept

13. Despite her degree in psychology, she could not find a job as a psychologist.
    a) employment
    b) a patient
    c) a supervisor

14. Astrologers believe that the movement of the stars influences our lives. They study the stars to <u>predict</u> the future.
    a) travel to
    b) depend on
    c) forecast

15. When the medium at the seance looked in the mirror, she did not see her own reflection. Instead, the mirror <u>projected</u> an image of the old man who was speaking through her.
    a) calculated
    b) presented
    c) explained

16. Scientists <u>challenge</u> the existence of the supernatural.
    a) dispute
    b) accept
    c) prove

17. The objects flew about the room with such <u>energy</u> and clear direction that I could only imagine they were flung about by a poltergeist.
    a) electricity
    b) attitude
    c) power

18. Despite the fact that the psychic claimed to have tele-pathic powers, the investigators <u>exposed</u> him as a fraud.
    a) revealed
    b) hid
    c) trusted

19. I imagine that psychokinesis would require great <u>mental</u> effort.
    a) psychological
    b) physical
    c) nervous

20. Nothing fell from the table because, although it had levitated about five centimetres above the floor, the table remained <u>stable</u>.
    a) uncertain
    b) balanced
    c) variable

Exercise B
Pronunciation—Syllables and Stress

Listen to your teacher or an audio dictionary to hear the pro-nunciation for each word in the list. Repeat each word aloud. Mark the syllables and major word stress.

1. approach (v): ap / **proach**
2. challenge (n): _____
3. conclusion (n): _____
4. dimensions (n): _____
5. energy (n): _____
6. exposure (n): _____
7. final (adj): _____
8. function (v): _____
9. indicate (v): _____
10. investigation (n): _____
11. involved (v): _____
12. items (n): _____
13. job (n): _____
14. labour (n): _____
15. mental (adj): _____
16. perceived (v): _____
17. predicted (v): _____
18. project (v): _____
19. reliance (n): _____
20. stability (n): _____

Exercise C
Word Forms

Fill in each blank with the word form indicated in parentheses. More than one word may be possible for each indicated word form.

1. approach (v): _____ (adj)
2. challenge (n): _____ (adj)
   _____ (v)
3. conclusion (n): _____ (v)
   _____ (adj)
4. energy (n): _____ (adj)
   _____ (adv)
5. exposure (n): _____ (v)
   _____ (adj)
6. final (adj): _____ (adv)
7. function (v): _____ (adj)
   _____ (adv)
8. indicate (v): _____ (n)
9. investigation (n): _____ (v)
10. involved (v): _____ (n)
11. items (n): _____ (v)

12. mental (adj): _____ (n)
    _____ (adv)
13. perceived (v): _____ (n)
14. predicted (v): _____ (adj)
    _____ (adv)
15. project (v): _____ (n)
16. reliance (n): _____ (n)
    _____ (v) _____ (adj)
17. stability (n): _____ (adj)

Exercise D

In a dictionary, find one example sentence for each word in Exercise A and copy it into your notebook. Draft a second sentence of your own. Then, work with a partner to revise and edit your sentence.

Exercise E

Read the following story and complete each blank with one of the words from the list. You do not have to change the grammatical form of any of the words. Use each word only once.

The Office Apparition

challenge	job	projects
energy	labour	rely
involved		

approached	exposed	investigate
concluded	indicated	perception
dimension		

It was ten o'clock on a Friday evening and I was just leaving the office. I was tired and had little 1 _____ left after such a long day at work. I had just started my new 2 _____ as a communications specialist the previous month, and I was eager to show that I liked my work. The job was interesting. I was 3 _____ in two major team 4 _____ and there were several problems we had to solve on a daily basis. I liked the 5 _____ of solving problems. It was my first job after graduating from college and even though I still lived at home with my parents, I liked that I didn't have to 6 _____ on my parents for money anymore. I was getting paid for my 7 _____ and becoming more independent.

finally	functioning	items

The building was quiet at this time of night, but I wasn't afraid. The building was very secure and well lit. Besides, the night security staff had already come by my office several times to check on me. I cleared my desk of my papers and was organizing my pens, pencils, and other small 8 _____ when my computer screen started doing some strange things. The screen started flashing and I thought I heard a faint cry. 9 _____, the screen went blank and the computer stopped 10 _____ altogether. It just stopped working. That wasn't too strange I guess. It wasn't the first time a computer crashed. But that faint cry didn't stop and I realized that it was coming from outside my office.

As I 11 _____ the open door to my office, it shut suddenly. Now I was afraid, but I was determined to 12 _____ where the faint cry was coming from. As I opened the door, I was sure that, from the corner of my eye, I saw a young girl running across the hall. She wasn't really running, she was floating. She didn't look quite real, though. There was a strange light around her body. She looked more like an apparition than a little girl. At first I thought my 13 _____ might be distorted, but then I saw her again. I tried to make sense of it all. The events that had just happened—the computer crashing, the faint cry, the door slamming shut, and this young girl floating across the hall—all 14 _____ that something mysterious was going on and I 15 _____ that what I had just seen was a ghost. Suddenly I wasn't afraid anymore because I had had paranormal experiences before although I had never been 16 _____ to a ghost. Still I've always believed that the material world is only one 17 _____ of life and that an active spiritual world exists too.

mentally	predicted	stable

I'm not an irrational person and I don't experience the extreme positive and extreme negative emotions that some of my friends do. My emotions don't control my actions. On the contrary, I have a very logical mind and I'm 18 _____ very 19 _____. I have had some clairvoyant instances in my life where I could tell what was going to happen in the future, but I had not

20 _____ that I would see a ghost this early in my new career. Still, I liked the idea of working with a ghost. This job was going to be even more interesting than I thought. So, I went back into my office, gathered together my belongings and headed out of the building. As I passed by the hall where I had seen my little ghost, I called out, "See you on Monday!"

Unit 3
The Road Less Travelled

ADJECTIVE ORDER

Exercise A

Categorize the adjectives in the five sentences below according to the descriptors in the chart. Note that not all categories are contained in every sentence.

EXAMPLE: Many medium-sized, ancient stone figures are found in Korea.

1. They found a single, small, intricately carved black onyx fertility statue.

2. She described the "Three Sisters" in Australia's Blue Mountains as three colossal, majestic, pointy blue-hazed peaks.

3. Hundreds of small, pristine, crystal-clear lakes make it a perfect vacation destination.

4. Countless interesting, rust-coloured Aboriginal religious drawings cover the base of Ayers Rock.

5. Their large, formerly grand, ancient dome-shaped temples dot the landscape.

Korean grandfather stone

	DETERMINER	SIZE	GENERAL DESCRIPTION	AGE	SHAPE	COLOUR	MATERIAL	ORIGIN	PURPOSE
EXAMPLE	many	medium-sized		ancient			stone		
1									
2									
3									
4									
5									

Exercise B

Complete the following paragraph by writing the adjectives in parentheses in the appropriate order in the spaces provided.

New Zealand is the ideal destination for 1 _____ (adventurous, all) nature lovers. The Routeburn Trail, located on the northern perimeter of the South Island, is a 2 _____ (scenic, moderately long) hike for young and old alike who wish to enjoy the breathtaking views that nature presents. 3 _____ (curving, man-made, narrow) paths snake through dense areas of forest. Periodic 4 _____ (natural, small) clearings provide a welcome rest stop to drop 5 _____ (heavy, waterproof) backpacks, sit back, and listen to the 6 _____ (unusual, countless) noises from birds and animals in the surrounding foliage. The trail winds its way to the 7 _____ (sandy, white, vast) beach on several occasions, allowing the weary hiker to dip tired toes in the refreshing ocean. And just when exhaustion is setting in, there is a 8 _____ (large, wood, ten-year-old) cabin where hikers can spend a dry, rejuvenating night before setting off on another day's journey.

Exercise C

Write phrases to describe the objects shown in the photographs.

1. Bonhomme (Quebec Winter Carnival mascot)

_____

_____

2. tree

_____

_____

3. mask

_____

_____

4. warrior

_____

_____

5. The Alps

_____

_____

Grammar in Use

Exercise D

Advertisements are full of descriptive phrases enticing us to purchase products or services. Read the following descriptions and try to identify the product being sold.

1. "floating twin blades flex to fit your curves"
   _____

2. "it's all-beef, nutritious, and used by top breeders throughout the country" _____

3. "smooth, creamy, and calorie-reduced—perfect for those hot days" _____

4. "quickly cuts through the grease to leave a sparkling shine" _____

5. "a light, refreshing, quenching taste"
   _____

6. "colourfast, washable, drip-dry" _____

7. "coated non-stick surface needs no oil"
   _____

8. "it leaves your skin feeling clean and soft"
   _____

9. "top-quality—one coat is guaranteed to cover in a single application" _____

10. "it's so lifelike it cries and wets its diaper"
    _____

One Step Beyond—Create an Activity

Exercise E

Write five product descriptions and see if your classmates can identify the products.

Exercise F

Your team of three or four is made up of promotion coordinators representing several fabulous resorts. In your promotional magazine, you want to describe the different resort destinations vividly in order to attract clientele. Your team will write four detailed descriptions for the following types of resorts:

1. Relaxing

2. Fun For the Whole Family

3. Exciting

4. Educational

Put your vacation getaway descriptions together to form a travel brochure. Copy the brochure for the other teams. Each class member will select the vacation that most appeals to him or her based on the descriptions provided.

Vocabulary

Exercise A

In the paragraph below, underline the synonyms or expressions that have the same meaning as the following words. Write the word above its underlined synonym.

| dangerous | magnificent | smooth |
| expert | renowned | traditional |

Pasquale Scaturro is a famous explorer who enjoys tackling perilous landscapes in order to challenge his adventurous spirit. Never one to take a conventional trip to touristy destinations, Scaturro has been to many remote locations. He is a skilful adventurer and has filmed some of the most outstanding scenery ever viewed by mankind. He has captured images of undisturbed waters in remote areas, as well as icy snowcaps on mountain tops.

Exercise B

Complete the following chart with the parts of speech listed, then write a sentence for each word that demonstrates its meaning. Note that it may not be possible to form every part of speech in every case.

Noun	Verb	Adjective	Adverb
		dangerous	
		expert	
		magnificent	
		renowned	
		smooth	
		traditional	

Exercise C

Replace the italicized words in the following sentences with more precise descriptive words.

1. Toronto is a *very large, beautiful* city. _____

_____

2. I thought that the Sydney Opera House was a *beautiful* building. _____
_____

3. The food in Spain was *good*. _____
_____

4. The people in Thailand were *nice*. _____

5. I saw ivory carvings in a Taiwanese museum that were *small* and *beautiful*. _____
_____

6. The Indonesian dancers were *good*. _____
_____

7. Her tour guide is *nice-looking*. _____
_____

8. The plane trip was *okay*. _____
_____

9. The mountain water was *cold*. _____
_____

10. France was *interesting*. _____
_____

Vocabulary Expansion 1

Descriptions are often made vivid by comparing something unknown to something with which the reader might be familiar. The degree of similarity can be emphasized using adverbs that intensify the adjective or adverb (intensifiers).

EXAMPLE: Australia is **considerably** larger than New Zealand.

Some useful expressions are

small difference   a bit
slightly
somewhat
much
substantially
large difference   considerably

Exercise D
Compare the following subjects using an intensifier.

1. Switzerland / Mexico
_____

2. Thai food / Indonesian food
_____

3. Japanese bullet train / express train
_____

4. first class / economy airline seats
_____

5. temperature in southern Colombia / temperature in Ecuador
_____

Grammar Focus 2

RELATIVE CLAUSES
Exercise A

Fill in the blanks with an appropriate relative pronoun. More than one answer may be possible.

Gloria had just graduated from university when she decided to take some time to explore exotic parts of the world ₁ _____ she was unfamiliar with. Her first stop was Australia, ₂ _____ is known for its koala bears and kangaroos. She travelled around Australia with some Brits ₃ _____ she had met on the plane. Together they travelled up the coast to Queensland. There, on the Great Barrier Reef, ₄ _____ is the largest living organism in the world, they learned to scuba dive. She still has fond memories of hitchhiking up the coast to Kakadu National Park, ₅ _____ is home to incredible wildlife. Her next stop was New Zealand, ₆ _____ is made up of three main islands. Each island has its own unique characteristics. New Zealanders and tourists ₇ _____ love to go hiking have many excellent trails to choose from. Gloria managed to make it through a couple of tough but spectacular trails. From there it was on to Southeast Asia—that was a whole new ball game!

Note: Traditionally, it was not acceptable to end a sentence with a preposition as in the first sentence of this paragraph. In formal writing it is still not acceptable; however, in informal writing it is quite common.

Exercise B

Combine the following sentences using relative clauses. Remember to use appropriate punctuation if the clause is non-restrictive.

1. Barb flew to Thailand. She had never been out of Canada.
_____

2. She met her sister there. Her sister had been living in Japan.

_____

_____

3. They enjoyed the food. It was hot and spicy.

_____

_____

4. They slept in guest houses. The guest houses were clean, cheap, and comfortable.

_____

_____

5. She bought a beautiful tapestry in the market at a good price. She had haggled over the price.

_____

_____

6. Barb rode an elephant while trekking in northern Thailand. The elephant could carry two people.

_____

_____

7. The sisters had a great time. They had a lot of catching up to do.

_____

_____

8. They saw some traditional dancers. The dancers were very skilled and graceful.

_____

_____

9. The temples were awe-inspiring. The temples were extremely ornate.

_____

_____

10. It was a great experience. She will probably never have the opportunity to repeat it.

_____

_____

Exercise C

Complete the following sentences about your travel habits.

1. I am someone who

_____

_____

2. I enjoy visiting places that

_____

_____

3. I like to try foods which

_____

_____

4. I don't enjoy seeing children who

_____

_____

5. The only country that

_____

_____

6. I take photographs that

_____

_____

7. I try to find locations where

_____

_____

8. I would never spend summertime in a country where

_____

_____

Grammar Expansion

Relative pronouns can be eliminated from sentences if the pronoun functions as an object in the sentence, or if the main verb or auxiliary in the relative clause is *be*.

EXAMPLES: The pen pal **that** I wrote to for the last ten years is coming to visit me.

The pen pal I wrote to for the last ten years is coming to visit me.

The girl **who is** watching TV is my sister.

The girl watching TV is my sister.

Exercise D

If possible, cross out the relative pronouns or relative pronouns + *be* in the following sentences. Be prepared to explain why you chose to eliminate them.

1. Have you seen the movie that Steven Spielberg made?

2. I am the person whom the lyrics are referring to.

3. Anyone who has ever seen the movie will agree.

4. Everyone who is invited is expected to attend.

5. The boy that I borrowed the pen from is absent today.

6. I saw a movie that you are sure to like.

7. It is the smell of fresh paint which gives her a headache.

8. I saw the band which you told me about last weekend.

Exercise E

The following reading details Pasquale Scaturro's adventures climbing Mount Everest.

Underline at least five relative clauses in this passage. Write an R above each restrictive clause and an NR above each non-restrictive clause. Draw a circle around the noun being modified.

Summiting Mount Everest

At 8,848 metres, Mount Everest, which is located on the border between Nepal and China, is the highest peak in the world. Since first being conquered in 1953 by Sir Edmund Hillary, who was a New Zealand 5 mountaineer and explorer, and his Sherpa mountaineer Tenzing Norgay, many have tried and failed to climb the mighty mountain. While over 200 climbers have lost their lives on the rugged terrain, approximately 2,500 have succeeded.

10 Pasquale Scaturro—who is the founder and president of Exploration Specialists, an international geophysical and exploration company—made his first attempt to climb Mount Everest in 1995, when he got all the way to the South Summit, at 8,750 metres. 15 Unfortunately, the final 100 metres of the mountain proved to be too dangerous. This portion of the climb required traversing an extremely treacherous exposed ridge, where one wrong step would send climbers plunging either 2,400 metres or 3,050 metres to their 20 deaths, and then climbing a challenging 12-metre rock wall. Because of the severe weather conditions, his team had to turn around. During the descent, they helped save the life of a woman who had collapsed in the snow and was in serious distress. They wrapped her in extra 25 clothing to try to keep her warm and used ropes to transport her hundreds of metres down the mountain—a challenging feat which probably saved her life.

Pasquale Scaturro made his second attempt to summit Mount Everest in 1998, with the Everest 30 Environmental Expedition, which was a group of climbers dedicated to preserving the natural environment. With no outside funding or guides, this group of dedicated environmentalists committed to cleaning up debris that had been left by previous climbers on both 35 the southeast ridge route and at the base camp. Both Scaturro and the Everest Environmental Expedition managed to achieve their goals. Scaturro realized his goal of reaching the summit of Mount Everest, and the team managed to carry off a lot of oxygen bottles, bat-40 teries, trash, and human waste that had been left on the mountain face by previous adventurers.

It was Scaturro's third attempt that brought him the most notoriety. Funded by the National Federation of the Blind, which pledged $250,000 to sponsor the 45 climb, Scaturro led an adventurous team on a record-breaking ascent that took several months: he climbed Mount Everest with a climber who was the first legally blind person to ever make an attempt. They reached the summit on May 25, 2001. The expedition was the cover 50 feature of the June 2001 issue of *Time* magazine, which called it one of the most successful Mount Everest expeditions in history. The climb set several Everest climbing records, including the first blind person to ever scale the mountain. They also summited the largest number 55 of climbers (19) from a group in a single day. In addition to Erik Weihenmayer, who was the blind climber, this group included the 64-year-old Sherman Bull, who was the oldest man to climb Everest, and Sherman's son Brad. They were also the first father-and-son team to 60 summit at the same time. The challenging exploits of this record-breaking climb are detailed in Erik Weihenmayer's book, *Touch the Top of the World* and the 2003 movie *Farther Than the Eye Can See.*

Exercise F

Write descriptive sentences about the following.

EXAMPLE: Mount Everest

Mount Everest, which is the highest mountain in the world, continues to challenge climbers.

1. climbers

_____

_____

2. the Everest Environmental Expedition

_____

_____

3. garbage

_____

_____

4. weather

_____

_____

5. Sherpas

_____

_____

6. book

_____

_____

7. climbing records

_____

_____

8. Erik Weihenmayer

_____

_____

Vocabulary Expansion 2

Exercise A

Read the following fictional interview and try to determine the meaning of the underlined idioms. Write a brief definition for each idiom.

Reporter: You really put your life <u>on the line</u> on your wilderness adventure. Was the potential danger part of the thrill?

Kathy Kucan: My husband and I knew that we would face many challenges on our survival trip, but we were determined to <u>give it our best shot</u>.

Reporter: Why did you decide to take the survival course first instead of just <u>playing it by ear</u>?

Kathy: We knew we had to learn how to deal with hardships and the unknown. We thought the course would be a mini trial of what we might face when we went travelling through Asia.

Reporter: What were some of the biggest challenges you faced?

Kathy: I had to find and cut down enough pine boughs for our group—the boughs weren't always easy to reach or cut through.

Reporter: Did you ever consider giving up and calling for your teacher to help?

Kathy: Well, by the end of our hike and the challenge of building the shelter, we were <u>on our last legs</u>, but we managed to get the shelter up and stay somewhat warm throughout the night.

Reporter: I'm sure that when you looked at the makeshift shelter that was supposed to keep you warm for the night you must have thought about turning around and heading home to a nice warm hotel room.

Kathy: That's true, but we were so close to achieving our goal that we didn't want to <u>blow it</u> by giving up then.

Reporter: Well Kathy, I have a lot of respect for you. I could certainly never have survived in the wilderness even for one night, nor would I really have wanted to. You know what they say—<u>different strokes for different folks</u>!

1. on the line

_____

2. give it one's best shot

_____

3. play it by ear

_____

4. on one's last legs

_____

5. blow it

_____

6. different strokes for different folks

_____

Exercise B

Complete the following sentences with the idioms from Exercise A. (You may need to change the pronoun.)

1. We aren't really sure where we are going on our vacation. We thought we'd just get in the car and

   _____

2. I know they say _____, but do you honestly know anyone in his right mind who would pierce his tongue?

3. Despite an acute attack of stage fright, the actor went out and _____

4. The car is _____. I'm not sure it will make it all the way to Florida.

5. The prime minister put his career _____ with his innovative election campaign in which he promised to quit his office if he didn't reduce the deficit to zero within three years.

6. This deal is crucial in determining if the company will stay afloat or go bankrupt, so please don't

   _____

Writing

The Descriptive Paragraph

The descriptive paragraph describes a person, event, object, feeling, or scene. The written words are used like an artist's paints, recreating an image for others. What is described and the type of words used to evoke a vivid picture depend on the topic and purpose of the paragraph. Descriptive paragraphs are very common in writing such as travel literature, science reports, police reports, and doctors' notes.

An effective descriptive paragraph

- creates a vivid visual picture with words.
- is arranged in a logical order (generally spatially).
- includes only those aspects and details that support the controlling idea in the topic sentence.
- uses vivid descriptive language that appeals to the senses to support the controlling idea in the topic sentence.
- indicates the attitude of the writer towards the subject.
- uses spatial transitional expressions to show place or position (such as at the top, under, to the left, on the right, beneath, or next to).

Exercise A

When travelling, Marco loved to jot down vivid descriptions of places he visited on whatever scraps of paper he could find stuffed in his pockets. He wrote on napkins, ticket stubs—even toilet paper, when desperate. Help Marco write a paragraph describing the Sydney Opera House to submit to a popular travel magazine. Eliminate any sentences that do not support the topic sentence. You will have to supply some of your own information and transitional sentences.

Topic Sentence: The Sydney Opera House, which opened in 1974, is a prime example of splendid architecture set on a background of inner-city beauty.

In front are the trendy cafés where a mosaic of people lounge around drinking their espressos.

Opera music can be truly inspirational, although some say it is an acquired taste.

Sydney is located in the state of New South Wales.

Behind the building, on the walkway, a band is busking for shelter money.

Framing the Opera House, slightly to the left, is the picturesque Sydney Harbour Bridge.

To the right of the Opera House, you can see magnificent botanical gardens with their exotic flora.

Australia is a former British penal colony.

The Opera House itself, with its unique curved designs, juts out into the harbour.

_____
_____
_____
_____
_____
_____
_____
_____
_____
_____
_____
_____
_____

Exercise B

Use the following points to write a paragraph describing the town of Banff.

Topic Sentence: As you look down Main Street towards the hotel in Banff, Alberta, you can't help but admire the beauty of this small quaint town nestled at the base of scenic mountains.

To the left	• the local pub • brightly painted • frequented by both locals and tourists
On the right	• grocery store and drug store • there many years • friendly staff
Down the centre	• stately streetlight standards • separate directions of traffic • romantic night atmosphere
At end of street	• hotel resort • full of tourists • spectacular views
Behind the hotel	• mountains • rising majestically • dwarf the hotel
Bottom of the mountain	• stately pines • reach for the sky • dense
Middle of the mountain	• scrub • sparse • brown
Mountain peak	• rocky • distant

Exercise C

Imagine that you are Pasquale Scaturro. You are writing to your wife, describing Gordon Brown to her. Use your imagination to create a complete picture with words.

Note: When describing a person, you may want to describe some or all of the following: facial appearance, body shape, fitness, mannerisms, habits, or knowledge of the expedition.

Exercise D

Editing

The following paragraph is very choppy and difficult to read because it contains too many short sentences and repeated words. Rewrite the paragraph, combining sentences with relative clauses where possible.

The warm atmosphere created by Santa Fe's friendly, diverse people and rich traditions matches the warmth of the climate. Santa Fe's mosaic comprises a variety of backgrounds. Some Santa Feans are Native American. Native Americans' ancestors have been in northern New Mexico for at least a thousand years. Some Santa Feans are the descendants of the Spanish conquistadors. The Spanish conquistadors came north from Mexico in the 16th century. The two cultures share a love and respect for the land. The two cultures share a deep respect and love for the traditions that have been passed down from generation to generation. Santa Feans are friendly. Santa Feans have always been accepting of different cultures. As a consequence, people from all walks of life feel welcomed. Santa Fe is located in the desert. Santa Fe is very warm. Santa Fe is a great place to visit because of the people and the atmosphere.

Exercise E

Think about the most breathtaking scene you can remember that made you wish you had a camera close at hand. The only means you have of sharing your vision with anyone is through your detailed description. Write a paragraph describing the scene. Use the following Descriptive Paragraph Checklist to edit your work.

☑ Descriptive Paragraph Checklist

- ☐ Have I considered my audience and purpose?
- ☐ Have I narrowed my topic?
- ☐ Does my topic sentence indicate the nature and importance of my description?
- ☐ Have I organized my paragraph spatially?
- ☐ Are the sentences and ideas arranged logically?
- ☐ Have I used spatial transitional expressions adequately and appropriately?
- ☐ Have I used enough vivid descriptions to create a clear picture in my reader's mind?
- ☐ Have I checked each sentence to make sure the order of my adjectives is correct?
- ☐ Have I eliminated short, choppy sentences and repetition where possible?
- ☐ Have I checked my paragraph to make sure the meaning of each sentence is clear?
- ☐ Have I checked my paragraph to make sure that I have used precise words and the correct form of words?
- ☐ Have I proofread my paragraph for errors in grammar, punctuation, and spelling?

Academic Word List

benefit	ensure	section
civil	equation	security
components	equivalent	similar
consistent	facilitate	site
cultural	imposed	source
distinction	interaction	techniques
dominant	perspective	

Exercise A

Word meaning

Match each definition in Column A with the appropriate sample sentence in Column B.

Column A

Part 1

1. regards as equivalent
2. makes certain
3. compatible
4. distinct part of something
5. position or location
6. be helped by something
7. communications between two or more people
8. made possible
9. protection
10. impressive due to great size

Part 2

11. having a unique quality
12. way of doing an activity
13. main / most important
14. in agreement with acceptable social standards
15. origin
16. having a likeness
17. relating to shared values and beliefs of a society
18. parts of a system or thing
19. mental view or outlook
20. something that is equal in value

Column B

a) Their positive experience is **consistent** with the experiences of other travellers in Laos.
b) The rafters had some very friendly **interactions** with the Sudanese.
c) The soldiers who **facilitated** the crossing were friendly.
d) Mount Everest is an **imposing** mountain.
e) The **section** of the trip through Sudan was difficult.
f) The rafters carried guns for **security**.
g) Scaturro **equates** climbing Everest with rafting the Nile.
h) We carefully selected a protected **site** where we could pitch our tent.
i) They will continue to **benefit** from their survival lessons.
j) Careful planning **ensures** a safe trip.

k) Arabic is the **dominant** language in Egypt.
l) The rapids are **similar** to those found in New Zealand.
m) The **source** of the Nile is a small stream.
n) The various **components** were carefully researched before the trip.
o) Climbing is an **equivalent** challenge to rafting unknown rapids.
p) They were scared by the **distinctive** howl of a wolf in the night.
q) The survival **techniques** they learned were very useful.
r) From his **perspective**, every adventure is worth trying.
s) The team was invited to take part in **cultural** festivities.
t) They were lucky that the people were **civil,** rather than hostile.

Exercise B

Pronunciation—Syllables & Stress

Listen to your teacher or an audio dictionary to hear the pronunciation for each word in the list. Repeat each word aloud. Mark the syllables and major word stress.

1. benefit (v): **bĕn** / e / fit
2. civil (adj): _____
3. components (n): _____
4. consistent (adj): _____
5. cultural (adj): _____
6. distinction (n): _____
7. dominant (adj): _____
8. ensure (v): _____
9. equation (n): _____
10. equivalent (n): _____
11. facilitate (v): _____
12. imposed (v): _____
13. interaction (n): _____
14. perspective (n): _____
15. section (n): _____
16. security (n): _____
17. similar (adj): _____
18. site (n): _____
19. source (n): _____
20. techniques (n): _____

Exercise C

Word Forms

Fill in each blank with the word form indicated in parentheses. More than one word may be possible for each indicated word form.

1. benefit (v): _____ (adj)

2. civil (adj): _____ (n)
    _____ (adv)

3. consistent (adj): _____ (n)
    _____ (adv)

4. cultural (adj): _____ (adj)

5. distinction (n): _____ (adj)
    _____ (adv)

6. dominant (adj): _____ (n)
    _____ (adv)

7. equation (n): _____ (v)

8. equivalent (n): _____ (n)

9. facilitate (v): _____ (n)

10. imposed (v): _____ (n)
    _____ (adj)

11. interaction (n): _____ (v)
    _____ (adv)

12. perspective (n): _____ (adj)

13. security (n): _____ (v)

14. similar (adj): _____ (n)
    _____ (adv)

15. techniques (n): _____ (adj)
    _____ (adv)

Exercise D

In a dictionary, find one example sentence for each word in Exercise A and copy it into your notebook. Draft a second sentence of your own. Then, work with a partner to revise and edit your sentence.

Exercise E

Read the following story and complete each blank with one of the words from the list. You do not have to change the grammatical form of any of the words. Use each word only once.

beneficial	distinct	interaction
civilization	ensures	perspectives
consistently	impose	source
cultures		

Since the beginning of 1 _____, mankind has had the desire to travel and explore other 2 _____. The resulting 3 _____ that occurs as people from different regions and backgrounds mix 4 _____ that individuals' world 5 _____ are broadened. This is very 6 _____ because as we learn about 7 _____ cultures, we learn to respect and accept differences. It is a lack of understanding of perceived differences that is often the 8 _____ of tension. Approaching new experiences with a 9 _____ positive attitude rather than trying to 10 _____ your own beliefs on other cultures is essential.

components	facilitator	similar
dominant	section	site
equate	secure	techniques
equivalent		

We decided to take the course so we could learn important 11 _____ to improve our chances of survival should we need to live in harsh conditions or circumstances 12 _____ to a natural disaster. The course was broken down into several 13 _____ that related to four 14 _____ aspects: preparation, health, food, and shelter. An expert 15 _____ taught us how to select a 16 _____ which is 17 _____ enough to pitch our tent. In another 18 _____ of the course we learned to find edible food in the wilderness that was 19 _____ to the minimum amount of nourishment needed to exist. We 20 _____ the lessons we learned in this course to some of the most useful things we have ever learned in our lives.

Unit 4
That's Not What I Meant

Vocabulary 1

Exercise A

Match all the definitions below to the correct idioms. One example has been done for you. Then create sentences for each idiom.

> to get someone to be precise
> to grasp the main idea of something
> to not understand
> to talk about something unrelated
> to get off topic
> to perceive the main argument
> to get distracted from main discussion point
> to comprehend
> to not get the main idea
> to hear a rumour
> to force a comment
> to make someone tell something
> ~~to understand~~
> to avoid saying something directly
> to move discussion away from the main topic
> to discover through gossip
> to talk around the main issue without stating it directly

Idioms	Meanings
a) to get the point of	_to understand_
b) to miss the point of	
c) to get sidetracked	
d) to beat around the bush	
e) to hear something through the grapevine	

f) to pin someone
down on something _____

Vocabulary Expansion

Exercise B

1. Read the passage below that describes how you can improve your listening skills for an intercultural work-place. Guess the meaning of the ten underlined idiomatic expressions. Or, if you wish, look them up in a dictionary.

In today's workplace, people from diverse cultures often work together. In North American culture, most people value speaking—which is seen as active—over listening—which is perceived as passive. In some other cultures, listening is valued more. If you want to build good relationships at work and be effective on the job, you'll need to listen up.

Here are some tips for becoming a more effective listener in intercultural interactions:

Know the speaker's purpose: Does the speaker want to <u>let off steam</u>, share information, solve a problem, or just <u>shoot the breeze</u>? Once you know the speaker's purpose, you'll be able to respond in a way that matches his or her expectations. That doesn't mean you'll tell the speaker what he or she wants to hear. It just means you'll both <u>be on the same page</u> in the conversation.

Keep interruptions to a minimum: Sometimes we <u>cut off</u> the speaker because we're really interested in what *we* have to say, not what our speaking partner has to say. Other times the conversation may be too slow for us and we want to <u>get to the point</u> more quickly. In North American culture, occasional interruptions are acceptable, but most of the time people regard excessive interrupters as rude, arrogant, and self-centred. As tempting as it may be to interrupt, you may be better off <u>biting your tongue</u>.

Don't let a speaker's style <u>turn you off</u>: Are you a fast talker? Do you speak loudly when you get excited? Do you have an indirect speaking style or do you like to get to the point? Individuals have different speaking styles. In a conversation, you may not have the same conversational style as your partner, and another speaker's style may turn you off. When that happens, don't <u>tune out</u>. Try to focus on what the person intends to say and not the person's way of speaking.

Show you are listening: How do you know when others are listening to you? Do they look out the window, tap their foot, or talk to you while they're reading their computer screen? Give other speakers your full attention. Let them know that you are <u>tuned in</u> to the conversation. In North American culture, leaning slightly forward into the conversation and maintaining direct eye contact are signals the listener is paying attention. People in different cultures may have different ways of signalling they are paying attention. In intercultural interactions, be careful about judging whether someone is paying attention to you based on eye contact.

Make sure you heard it right: Many misunderstandings could be avoided if we just got into the habit of <u>checking in</u> with the speaker to make sure that we've grasped the speaker's intended message. Expressions such as "Let me just make sure I understand what you're saying" or "If I understand you correctly, you said that…" go a long way to prevent misunderstandings.

2. Replace the underlined words in each sentence with a form of the expressions from the passage above. You may need to change the grammatical form of the expressions.

   a) I didn't think it wise to tell my boss his idea was terrible so I <u>stopped myself from saying anything</u>.

   b) I can't discuss drugs with my teenager because every time I bring up the subject, he <u>doesn't listen</u>.

   c) You have precisely three minutes to present your arguments. After three minutes, you will be <u>stopped from talking</u>.

   d) She complained for an hour about all the problems she was having with her boyfriend. She really needed to <u>get her angry feelings out</u>.

   e) The teacher has this annoying habit of clearing his throat when he speaks. It really <u>annoys me</u>.

   f) I can talk to my sister on the phone for hours. We don't have anything important to say to each other. We just <u>talk about unimportant stuff</u>. It's relaxing.

   g) Okay, class, <u>pay attention</u>! There's going to be a test.

   h) Petra and Bill <u>had the same perspective</u> when it came to planning their honeymoon.

   i) She spoke in a very emotional manner. It was clear she needed to <u>talk about what was bothering her</u>.

   j) Stop talking in circles and <u>say what you mean</u>.

3. Write a dialogue using at least three of the expressions. Be prepared to perform the dialogue for your class with a partner.

Grammar Focus 1

CONJUNCTIONS AND PREPOSITIONS OF CONTRAST

Exercise A

Fill in each blank with an appropriate contrasting word or phrase from the list below. Use each word only once.

although	even though	while
but	in spite of the fact that	yet
despite	whereas	

1. _____ Jasmine has been learning English for six years, she still has difficulty communicating with English speakers.

2. His words say he is not angry, _____ his gestures say he is.

3. _____ having attended the Effective Listening workshop at his company, Carlos remains a poor listener.

4. Maria doesn't believe she communicates well in English _____ many of her colleagues have commented on her good grasp of the language.

5. Ken is always trying to improve his communication skills _____ his wife makes no effort to improve her skills.

6. Professor Acker usually gets to the point quickly in her lectures _____ Professor Ramirez notoriously beats around the bush.

7. Manuela doesn't think she can write English very well _____ she can write a simple letter or short note.

One Step Beyond—Create an Activity

Exercise B

Write eight sentences, using a conjunction or preposition of contrast in each. Then rewrite each sentence, leaving out the expression of contrast. Exchange your activity with a classmate and fill in the blanks.

Vocabulary 2

Exercise A

Each sentence below contains a word which does not make sense in its context. Underline the incorrect word and replace it with an appropriate form of one of the following words.

barrier   gesture   message
concise   interact   perceive
cue   interpersonal   vague
feedback

1. Good business writing should not be wordy; it must be clear and challenging.

2. Although she had difficulty handling the tasks of the job, her photocopying skills were excellent; consequently, she was well-liked by her colleagues.

3. Her poor listening skills remained a serious supervisor to her communication.

4. Ten minutes into his presentation, he noticed that people in the audience were beginning to fidget and make noise. Unfortunately, he didn't recognize that these were computers that people were losing interest in what he was saying.

5. The conversation became frustrating for Janet because Neil was very lazy about what he had expected. She wanted to pin him down on the specifics.

6. Steven enjoyed working for Soraya because she offered constructive paper about his work.

7. With a nod of her head, she wrote for him to stop talking.

8. Her training in group dynamics has made her a very inappropriate team player.

9. The success of this television talk show, in which viewers call the station to ask questions of celebrities, is attributed to its unfortunate format.

10. "I'm sorry, Mrs. Reiss isn't in at the moment. Would you like to leave a briefcase?"

Grammar Focus 2

TRANSITION WORDS AND PHRASES OF CONTRAST

Exercise A

Use a transition word from the list below to join the contrastive ideas in the following sentences. Remember to use appropriate punctuation.

even so   nonetheless   on the other hand
however   on the contrary   still
nevertheless

1. Marjorie finds it difficult to confront people.
   She confronted her supervisor about an unacceptable comment.

   _____

   _____

2. John doesn't believe that criticizing the work of others is bad business practice.
   He believes constructive criticism is a good way to help people do their jobs better.

   _____

   _____

3. Dianne believes in giving constructive criticism.
   She doesn't like receiving constructive criticism.

   _____

   _____

4. Latin Americans often hug when saying hello.
   Germans usually shake hands.

   _____

   _____

5. People from countries such as Switzerland may appear reserved and aloof.
   They form close friendships with others.

   _____

   _____

6. Mr. Buhl has taught communications for three years.
   That doesn't mean he is an effective communicator himself.

   _____

   _____

7. Mrs. Lombardi believes in getting to the point. Sometimes she beats around the bush.

_____

_____

Exercise B
Putting it all together
Read the following essay and then answer the questions.

Communication and Success in the Workplace

As I consider how effective my colleagues are in their jobs, I realize that our communication styles greatly influence our success at work. Consider two employees—Elyse Meyers, Marketing Manager, and Marybeth
5 Armstrong, Accounting Manager—who work for the city tourism association. Elyse is an intelligent, well-educated woman dedicated to her work. She enjoys her work and supervises a staff of five. Marybeth is also intelligent and well-trained in her profession. She too
10 supervises a staff of five and enjoys her work. Their profiles seem similar, but whereas Elyse's staff members are happy in their jobs and feel their supervisor is effective, Marybeth's staff members complain that working for her is frustrating, and one worker is even consid-
15 ering resigning. Of course, there could be many reasons for the differences in how the workers feel, but one marked difference between these two groups is the communication style of the department managers.

Both managers set distinct tones when they began
20 in their respective departments. When Elyse became manager five years ago, she began by meeting privately with everyone in her department—"to get acquainted," she said. Then she met with her team as a group to set department goals and explain her expectations of the
25 department. Elyse religiously holds weekly department meetings in which the team members update each other on what's happening in their areas. Once a year, Elyse invites her colleagues to a two-day staff retreat—a think-tank, where they all brainstorm new marketing
30 initiatives and generally have a good time. Although they work hard from nine to five, they do manage to make time for recreation and fun. When Marybeth joined the company as manager three years ago, she was a bit unsure of how her colleagues would accept
35 her age. She was quite a bit younger than some of her staff members and, consequently, wanted to make sure that her staff respected her for her knowledge and skills. She sent out a lengthy memo outlining her visions for the department and invited staff to see her personally if
40 they wanted further clarification of her expectations. As

a result of her impersonal communication style, she and her staff got off on the wrong foot. Three years later, she still hasn't developed the same rapport with the accounting department staff that Elyse enjoys with the
45 marketing team. Marybeth writes a monthly update column for her department in the company newsletter which also keeps staff informed about company initiatives. Even so, Marybeth's staff feels isolated and left in the dark about what is happening in the department.
50 They complain that they aren't informed of department and company initiatives. Marybeth, in fact, is quite annoyed that her staff are not more informed about what's happening, considering that the information is available to them—the postscript on her column even
55 invites any company staff member to contact her for more information.

Others in the company have begun to notice the differences in the two departments. Six months ago, when the company president spoke to the two managers about 60 the differences in their departments' performance, Marybeth responded that her staff were simply not as motivated as the marketing people. "Besides," she claimed, "everyone knows that marketing people are outgoing, while accountants are number crunchers, pre-65 ferring to work alone with numbers rather than with people." Elyse, however, offered a different perspective and shared what she thought contributed to her team's success: effective communication. Marybeth quickly responded, confirming that she, too, communicates with 70 her staff through her monthly updates in the newsletter and her "open-door" policy. Although she agreed to look into reasons for the poor morale of workers in her department, she hasn't been able to find the source of the problem. "Besides," she thinks to herself, "I have so 75 much work to do. If I spend all my time holding everyone's hand, how will I ever get my work done?"

While Marybeth has spent her time with her nose to the ground, working hard to prove herself, Elyse has been busy building a productive team that communi-80 cates well and has implemented several innovative and successful marketing promotions. Elyse is confident that her career is on the upswing. And she is right; the company has just announced Elyse's appointment as Vice-President of Marketing. Marybeth, on the other 85 hand, is beginning to feel that her staff members don't respect her, and she knows they gossip about her, talking behind her back. When she took the position three years ago, she had hoped she could demonstrate her competence as a worker and a manager. Now, she won-90 ders if she'll have this job in six months' time.

While there are some Elyses out there in the world of work, there are probably more Marybeths. Many workers are determined to prove their competence as effective workers, managers, and company team mem-95 bers, yet they underestimate the importance of good communication and team-building in doing so. Among the skills North American employers say they look for in potential and promotable employees, communication consistently ranks in the top three in all major sur-100 veys. But, in spite of the fact that colleges and universities are placing greater emphasis on developing reading, writing, and listening skills, many of us do not excel in communicating effectively with others. On the contrary, we lack the communication skills needed 105 to work effectively with others. Perhaps we have misunderstood what good communication means; it means much more than speaking and writing English well. Effective communication requires a style of behaviour that promotes and encourages the clear 110 expression of ideas and knowledge. It is a skill that can be learned and, as illustrated in the case above, it has a great impact on our success in the workplace.

Locate the expressions below in the reading and write the line number for each in the parentheses provided. Then write the meaning of these expressions based on their context in the reading.

1. to set the tone: par. 2 (   )

   _____

   _____

2. (to do something) religiously: par. 2 (   )

   _____

   _____

3. to get off on the wrong foot: par. 2 (   )

   _____

   _____

4. to develop (or have) a good rapport with someone: par. 2 (   )

   _____

   _____

5. to feel (or be) left in the dark about something: par. 2 (   )

   _____

   _____

6. number cruncher: par. 3 (   )

   _____

   _____

7. open-door policy: par. 3 (   )

   _____

   _____

8. to hold someone's hand (handholding): par. 3 (   )

   _____

   _____

9. to talk behind someone's back: par. 4 (   )

   _____

   _____

Exercise C

1. Underline the four coordinating conjunctions of contrast (but / yet) in the reading.

2. Double underline at least five subordinate conjunctions of contrast (although / though / even though / while / whereas / in spite of the fact that / despite) in the reading.

3. Circle at least four transition words and phrases of contrast (however / still / nevertheless / nonetheless / on the contrary / even so / on the other hand).

Exercise D

1. Complete the following diagram to show the similarities (the shared part of the circles) and differences (the unique parts of the circles) between Elyse Meyers and Marybeth Armstrong. Then write five sentences that show the similarities, and five sentences that show the differences between the two managers. Use as many words and expressions of contrast as possible.

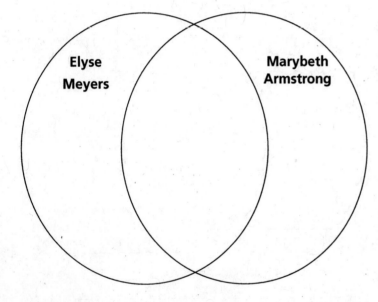

Exercise E

The connecting words and transitional expressions in some of the sentences below are incorrect. Put an *X* in the box beside each sentence with an inappropriate transitional expression or connecting word. Then rewrite the inappropriate sentences with appropriate connectors.

☐ 1. Children in the United States attend school for 180 days per year **and** students in Japan attend school 240 days per year.

☐ 2. Americans are friendly people; **on the contrary**, they don't like to be touched.

☐ 3. Monochronic people do one thing at a time; **nonetheless**, polychronic people do many things at once.

☐ 4. **Even so**, the same gesture can mean different things in different countries, the meaning of gestures can easily be learned.

☐ 5. **While** the top two cultural values of Americans are freedom and independence, the top values of Arabs are family security and family harmony.

☐ 6. People from different cultures may have dramatically different styles of communicating. **Even so**, it is possible to overcome cultural barriers to communicate effectively.

☐ 7. Latin Americans tend to build lifetime relationships, **in spite of the fact that** the British are accustomed to short-term relationships.

☐ 8. In Germany it is acceptable to talk about politics in casual conversation. In Mexico, **however**, this topic should be avoided.

☐ 9. **Although** the Japanese are sometimes hierarchical, placing great importance on age and seniority, they also value group consensus and cooperation.

☐ 10. Enrique adjusted quickly to his life in Australia. Diego, **yet**, experienced many months of frustration before he felt comfortable.

Exercise F

The sentences below express contrasts. Rewrite each sentence using different contrastive words and expressions without changing the meaning of the sentence. Pay attention to punctuation.

1. A bilingual child may speak English at school, but switch to Polish, Spanish, or Cantonese at home.

   a) yet: _____
   _____

   b) although: _____
   _____

   c) whereas: _____
   _____

2. In one study on bilingual education in New York City, researchers found that students who were taught most of their classes in English learned English well,

whereas students who were taught different subjects in their primary language did not learn English well.

a) while: _____

_____

b) however: _____

_____

c) on the other hand: _____

_____

3. Although it is more difficult to learn a second language in adulthood, it is not impossible.

a) even though: _____

_____

b) though: _____

_____

c) nonetheless: _____

_____

4. Even though Sari Kristiina moved to North America in her forties without having learned any English, she managed to learn English with native-like fluency.

a) even so: _____

_____

b) in spite of the fact that: _____

_____

c) still: _____

_____

Writing

Paragraphs that Compare and Contrast

Comparison and contrast paragraphs detail the similarities and differences between people, objects, or items, such as the similarities and differences in the communication styles of men and women. Similarly, a comparison and contrast paragraph can be used to show the advantages and disadvantages of each communication style. The purpose of writing such a paragraph is to persuade or inform the reader. There are two basic ways to organize a comparison and contrast paragraph. The first is to make **point-by-point comparisons**, and the second is to totally describe one item and then the other. The latter technique is known as the **block method**.

1. Point-by-point Comparison

In this type of writing, you address each comparative point from both perspectives before moving on to the next point.

For example, if you were comparing the communication styles of men and women, you would pick two or three main comparative points, such as language and directness, and then write about each point from the male perspective and then from the female perspective.

EXAMPLE:

Comparative Point	Perspective
1. language	- men use strong, aggressive language - women use softer language
2. directness	- men say exactly what they are thinking - women express their views indirectly, expecting the listener to decode what they really mean

This type of organization is useful when organizing complex topics. Points are clearly made because the reader is able to see the similarities and differences immediately.

2. The Block Method

Although the same points are discussed in this method as in the point-by-point method, the information is organized in blocks. For example, in the case of comparing men's and women's communication styles, you would write all about men's communication styles and then all about women's styles. The points of comparison are presented in the same order in each block and the reader must make the link between the points being compared or contrasted. This method is most useful for short pieces of writing, such as paragraphs and short essays, where the reader is able to easily remember all the information provided.

EXAMPLE:

Perspectives of Men Comparative Point	
1. language	- men use strong, aggressive language
2. directness	- men say exactly what they are thinking
Perspectives of Women Comparative point	
1. language	- women use softer language
2. directness	- women express their views indirectly, expecting the listener to decode what they really mean

Exercise A

Reread the essay "Communication and Success in the Workplace" and determine which method of organization the writer used when comparing and contrasting the communication styles of Elyse and Marybeth.

Exercise B

Using the information provided below, write a paragraph in which you compare the attributes of monochronic cultures to those of polychronic cultures. Use the block method of organization. Then use the Comparison and Contrast Paragraph Checklist that follows Exercise C to edit your work.

People from Monochronic Cultures	People from Polychronic Cultures
• Do one thing at a time	• Do many things at once
• Concentrate on a specific job	• Are highly distractible and subject to interruptions
• Take time commitments seriously	• View time commitments casually
• Are committed to their work	• Are committed to people
• Show respect for private property; rarely borrow or lend	• Borrow and lend things often
• Are accustomed to short-term relationships	• Tend to build life-long relationships

Rewrite the paragraph, this time using the point-by-point method of organization. Use the Comparison and Contrast Paragraph Checklist to edit your work.

One Step Beyond—Create an Activity

Exercise C

Draw a chart as in Exercise B, comparing two subjects of your choice. Exchange your chart with a classmate and write a comparison and contrast paragraph based on the information in your classmate's chart. Use the Comparison and Contrast Paragraph Checklist to edit your work.

☑ Comparison and Contrast Paragraph Checklist

☐ Have I considered my audience and purpose (to explain, to persuade, or to inform)?

☐ Have I narrowed my topic?

☐ Does my topic sentence state which items I am comparing and contrasting?

☐ Does my topic sentence indicate my main point (the purpose of my comparison)?

☐ Have I organized the paragraph either point-by-point or by the block method?

☐ Does my organization pattern suit the complexity of the topic?

☐ Have I chosen the most significant comparative and contrastive points to support the main point in my topic sentence?

☐ Do I use the same comparative and contrastive points and in the same sequence for each item of comparison?

☐ Have I used appropriate transitions to show similarities and differences?

☐ Have I checked my paragraph to make sure the meaning of each sentence is clear?

☐ Have I checked my paragraph to make sure that I have used precise words and the correct form of the words?

☐ Have I proofread my paragraph for errors in grammar, punctuation, and spelling?

Academic Word List

appropriate	interpretation	resources
consent	notion	sequence
contrast	parallel	status
ethnic	partnership	task
fundamental	previous	validity
implies	reaction	volume
instance	resolution	

Exercise A
Word Meanings

For each sentence below, choose the correct meaning of the underlined word.

1. In order to interpret a message <u>appropriately</u>, it is necessary to grasp the intention of the speaker.
   a) properly
   b) politely
   c) carelessly

2. Sociolinguist Deborah Tannen studies gender communication. She <u>contrasts</u> the communication styles of men and women.
   a) compares opposites
   b) compares similarities
   c) compares differences

3. Many communication problems between the sexes could be <u>resolved</u> if men and women understood the differences in their conversational styles.
   a) understood
   b) damaged
   c) fixed

4. In some cultures, raising the <u>volume</u> of your voice may indicate anger, while in others, it may signal that the speaker is passionate about the topic.
   a) loudness
   b) speed
   c) emotion

5. North American culture values equal relationships in communication, where differences in <u>status</u> are minimized.
   a) cultural background
   b) power positions
   c) intellectual ability

6. The <u>notion</u> that men and women have the same communication style is not supported by research.
   a) idea
   b) experience
   c) rejection

7. When a woman talks about her problems with a friend, it does not necessarily <u>imply</u> that she wants advice on how to fix the problem.
   a) cause
   b) lead to
   c) indicate

8. Differences in communication styles between men and women <u>parallel</u> the differences in behaviour patterns of men and women.
   a) are like
   b) are different from
   c) are cause for

9. The computer manual was confusing because the steps for setting up the computer were described in the wrong <u>sequence</u>.
   a) order
   b) category
   c) program

10. Most women in North America expect a marriage to be an equal <u>partnership</u>.
    a) human right
    b) romance
    c) relationship

11. Fiona expected her boyfriend to apologize and say "I am sorry." When she didn't hear those words, she <u>reacted</u> angrily.
    a) responded
    b) rejected
    c) refused

12. Many people believe that men and women are <u>fundamentally</u> the same, despite some differences in their conversational styles.
    a) absolutely
    b) basically
    c) never

13. The Internet has many <u>resources</u> for learning more about cross-cultural communications.
    a) abilities to improve
    b) kinds of information
    c) research about

14. In Canadian business practice, a company cannot share customer information with other businesses without the customer's <u>consent</u>.
    a) money
    b) information
    c) permission

15. There is considerable evidence that communication patterns differ not only among different gender groups but also different <u>ethnic</u> groups.

    a) cultural

    b) sex

    c) age

16. The conflict situation was an <u>instance</u> of miscommunication.

    a) conclusion

    b) example

    c) problem

17. <u>Previous</u> to taking a communications course in college, Sheila was not an effective listener.

    a) after

    b) at the time of

    c) before

18. The two students had different <u>interpretations</u> of the writer's intentions.

    a) understandings or explanations

    b) interests or motivations

    c) experiences or histories

19. Your interpretation is not <u>valid</u>. There is no logic or evidence for it.

    a) proper

    b) wrong

    c) legal

20. In this assignment, the teacher was unclear about the <u>tasks</u> she expected of the students.

    a) actions

    b) marking

    c) interest

Exercise B
Pronunciation—Syllables and Stress

Listen to your teacher or an audio dictionary to hear the pronunciation for each word in the list. Repeat each word aloud. Mark the syllables and major word stress.

1. appropriate (adj): ap / **prop** / ri / ate

2. consent (n): _____

3. contrast (v): _____

4. ethnic (adj): _____

5. fundamental (adj): _____

6. implies (v): _____

7. instance (n): _____

8. interpretation (n): _____

9. notion (n): _____

10. parallel (adj): _____

11. partnership (n): _____

12. previous (adj): _____

13. reaction (n): _____

14. resolution (n): _____

15. resources (n): _____

16. sequence (n): _____

17. status (n): _____

18. task (n): _____

19. validity (n): _____

20. volume (n): _____

Exercise C
Word Forms

Fill in each blank with the word form indicated in parentheses. More than one word may be possible for each indicated word form.

1. appropriate (adj): _____ (adv)

2. consent (n): _____ (v)
    _____ (adj)

3. contrast (v): _____ (n)
    _____ (adj)

4. ethnic (adj): _____ (n)

5. fundamental (adj): _____ (adj)

6. implies (v): _____ (n)
    _____ (adj)

7. instance (n): _____ (adj)
    _____ (adv)

8. interpretation (n): _____ (v)
    _____ (adj)

9. parallel (adj): _____ (v)
    _____ (n)

10. partnership (n): _____ (v)
    _____ (adj)

11. previous (adj): _____ (adv)

12. reaction (n): _____ (v)
    _____ (adj)

13. resolution (n): _____ (v)
    _____ (adj)

14. resources (n): _____ (adj)
15. sequence (n): _____ (v)
    _____ (adj) _____ (adv)
16. validity (n): _____ (v)
    _____ (adj)
17. volume (n): _____ (adj)

Exercise D

In a dictionary, find one example sentence for each underlined word in Exercise A and copy it into your notebook. Draft a second sentence of your own. Then, work with a partner to revise and edit your sentence.

Exercise E

Read the following story and complete each blank with one of the words from the list. You do not have to change the grammatical form of any of the words. Use each word only once.

appropriate	fundamental	partnerships
contrasted	interpretation	status
ethnic		

You can improve your communication skills by checking that your ₁ _____ of a speaker's message is ₂ _____ rather than just assuming you have understood correctly. Assuming that people will say what they mean directly is a ₃ _____ mistake. Deborah Tannen, for example, has found that when the communication styles of men and women are ₄ _____, men are more direct in some cases, while women are more indirect in some cases. The same is also true of different ₅ _____ groups. While one will find all different kinds of communication patterns within any cultural group, research shows that cultures generally value certain communication styles more than others. For example, in Japan, much more attention is given to the role of the ₆ _____ of people in conversation than in Canada. Communication partners will adjust their language and behaviour to accommodate differences in status. Canadians tend to value equal ₇ _____ in their personal and professional lives, and will behave accordingly. Also, in Canadian business communication, it is more common to get to the point quickly and directly than to spend a lot of time on chatting about personal issues.

| sequence | task |

Traditionally, North Americans have tended to be more ₈ _____-oriented than relationship oriented in their business dealings although the value of building good relationships is becoming more apparent. In some cultures, the ₉ _____ of communication topics in business interactions is different. In Arabic cultures, for example, people may spend a lot of time discussing family and personal things, and address business deals much later.

| appropriately | react |
| instance | resolve |

In cross-cultural business interactions, it is important to ₁₀ _____ ₁₁ _____ to these differences. Cultural and gender differences in communication styles can lead to misunderstandings. Of course it is important to ₁₂ _____ misunderstandings quickly, but it is preferable to avoid them in the first place. Every ₁₃ _____ of miscommunication is a potential source of conflict.

| notion | resources | valid |

The same communication patterns may imply different messages in different interactions and that is one reason that the study of communication differences in gender and culture has become such a popular topic. The ₁₄ _____ that all people are the same when it comes to communication styles does not appear to be ₁₅ _____ If you want to learn more about cross-cultural or gender communications, visit your local library or the Internet for many wonderful ₁₆ _____ on the subject.

Unit 5
The Cutting Edge

Grammar Focus 1

NOUN CLAUSES

Exercise A

Noun clauses often follow verbs of mental activity. (See Student Book, Grammar Appendix page 173.) Reread the article "Science Faction" and answer the following questions using noun clauses.

1. What surprising fact did you learn about the technologies portrayed in science fiction?

   I learned _____

   _____

2. What have you learned about how filmmakers ensure the technology portrayed in their shows is believable?

   I have learned _____

   _____

3. What have you realized about the impact science fiction has on science?

   I have realized _____

   _____

4. What are two new things that you learned about the technology portrayed in science fiction?

   I learned _____

   _____

5. What do you now believe about the gadgets portrayed in movies like *Total Recall* and *Minority Report*?

   I now believe _____

   _____

6. What role do you feel Hollywood plays in advancing technological development?

   I feel _____

   _____

Exercise B

The technological ideas portrayed in recent science-fiction movies are not really so unbelievable. In *Minority Report*, police officers used jet packs to fly around. This technology, developed by Bell Aerospace in Buffalo, New York, made its real-life debut in 1961 and was called the rocket-belt. It consisted of a small backpack propulsion unit developed by Wendell Moore. The backpack provided thrust power to lift an individual off the ground for a short 20-second hop, and 11 men have free-flown with this technology. Now, almost 50 years later, the US military is experimenting with a strap-on helicopter called the Solotrek, designed by an American company, Millennium Jet Inc. The pilot uses controls to drive two fans attached to a normal piston engine. If anything goes wrong, a parachute attached to a rocket brings the pilot and machine safely to earth. Although primarily targeted for military use, civilian use is not out of the question in the future.

Summarize the paragraph by filling in the blanks with noun clauses.

1. The jet packs that _____ are similar to the rocket-belt which debuted in 1961.

2. The fact that _____ didn't prevent 11 men from free-flying a rocket-belt.

3. Almost 50 years later, it turns out that

   _____.

4. If anything goes wrong, pilots are assured that

   _____.

Exercise C

Restate the objects of the following sentences using a noun clause that begins with a question word, and write the new sentences. The objects have been bolded for you.

EXAMPLE: Alicia doesn't know the **date** of the new movie's release.

   Alicia doesn't know **when the new movie is being released.**

1. Lee is unaware of the **location** of the filming.

   _____

   _____

2. You will be impressed by the **number of returning stars** we have signed.

   _____

   _____

3. Do you know her **reason for watching the show**?

   _____

   _____

4. Are you aware of the **timing** of the publicity campaign kickoff?

   _____

   _____

5. I can't identify the **best actor** on the show.

   _____

   _____

Exercise D

Complete the following sentences with a noun clause in the object position. Be careful of tense changes.

1. I like to watch reruns of classic science-fiction shows like *Star Trek* even though I've seen them all several times. This addiction, according to my best friend, is incomprehensible. He can't understand **why** _____

   _____

   _____

2. I explained **that** _____

   _____

3. He wanted to know **what** _____

   _____

4. He also wanted to know **how long** _____

   _____

5. I couldn't remember exactly **when** _____

   _____

6. I'm sure the show's creator, Gene Roddenberry, never knew **how** _____

   _____

7. Nor did Roddenberry envision **how** _____

   _____

8. I wonder if my friend will ever understand **what** _____

   _____

   _____

Grammar Expansion

In conversation, when responding affirmatively to a yes/no question, *so* can be used in place of the *that* clause after certain verbs such as *hope, think, believe, assume, be afraid, suppose, guess, imagine,* and the phrases *it appears,* and *it seems*.

EXAMPLE: Was the experiment a success?

I believe **so**. (so = that the experiment was a success)

A negative response can be formed by the negative verb + *so*, or the verb + *not*.

EXAMPLE: Was the experiment a success?

I **don't believe so**.

I **believe not**.

Note: The verbs *be afraid, guess,* and *hope* can only be followed by *not* in a negative sentence.

Exercise E

You are being interviewed by a local newspaper reporter. Respond to the reporter's questions with a negative or positive response, and substitute *so* for the *that* clause. Add another line to explain your response.

EXAMPLE: Reporter: Does sci-fi TV appeal to everyone?

You: I don't think so. I'm a huge fan but there are many people who think it's a waste of time.

Note: You could respond "I think not." However, when that construction is used with the verb *think*, it produces either a very formal, condescending tone or a sarcastic one.

1. R: Is it the futuristic nature of sci-fi shows that appeals to you?

   Y: _____

   _____

2. R: Would you still be interested in sci-fi shows if the high-tech gadgetry they portray didn't seem realistic?

   Y: _____

   _____

3. R: Do you think having scientists as consultants for sci-fi shows ensures that the futuristic technology is believable?

   Y: _____

   _____

4. R: Are all sci-fi shows well-written and well-produced?

   Y: _____

   _____

5. R: Will sci-fi shows continue to be popular for generations to come?

   Y: _____

   _____

6. R: Would you let your children watch a sci-fi movie at age eight?

   Y: _____

   _____

Grammar in Use

Exercise F

Underline the noun clauses in the following quotations. Then write a few sentences after each quotation, outlining your response to it. Use noun clauses or substitutes for noun clauses in your response.

That is really the glory of science—that science is tentative, that it is not certain, that it is subject to change.
— Isaac Asimov

_____

_____

_____

The real danger is not that computers will begin to think like men, but that men will begin to think like computers.
— Sydney J. Harris

_____

_____

_____

It was thought that technological advances would benefit mankind. Instead of saving work, (electrical "labour-saving") devices permit everybody to do his own work. What the 19th century had delegated to servants and housemaids, we now do for ourselves.
— Marshall McLuhan (paraphrased)

_____

_____

_____

Vocabulary 1

Exercise A

The following words are commonly found in readings related to science. Group the words under the appropriate headings.

analysis	examination	investigation
argument	example	observation
debate	experiment	research

Careful and Systematic Study	Thinking and Reasoning

Exercise B

In the following sentences, the writer has used incorrect prepositions after the vocabulary words from Exercise A. Cross out the incorrect bolded preposition and write the correct one above.

1. After a careful analysis **from** the data, the researcher drew her conclusions.

2. She presented an argument **with** hiring a scientist as a consultant for the movie.

3. They are scheduled to hold a debate **for** the appropriateness of making the study of science fiction in high school mandatory.

4. That is a clear example **for** the importance of reading science fiction.

5. A close examination **about** the movie reveals many influences of early sci-fi writers.

6. This is definitely an experiment **for** great consequence.

7. We conducted an investigation **for** the claims that time travel had been invented.

8. His observation **for** the night sky revealed a new planet.

9. Scientists continue to conduct research **from** growing human organs.

One Step Beyond—Create an Activity

Exercise C

Find an interesting newspaper article about science or technology. Rewrite the article leaving blanks for all prepositions that follow a noun. Then exchange your article with a partner, and fill in the appropriate prepositions in the new article.

Vocabulary Expansion

Exercise D

Read the following dialogue and try to determine the meaning of the bolded idioms from the context. Then think of situations in your own life when you might use some of these idiomatic expressions, and complete the chart below.

Reporter: The life of a scientist must be a very glamorous one.

Scientist: Not really. Funding is difficult to get and you are constantly **under pressure** to get results from your research. I spend many an evening poised over a microscope **burning the midnight oil**.

Reporter: Don't you have research assistants helping you?

Scientist: Sometimes—if I'm lucky. Regardless, I have to **roll up my sleeves and dig in**, in order to conduct my experiments. There is a lot of labour that goes into a project before anyone even hears about its existence.

Reporter: How do you **figure out** what is really relevant in your findings?

Scientist: Most important findings come from testing and re-testing to check for validity. There are certain guidelines to determine whether your findings are significant or not. It's possible to have worked for months only to **find out** that your results are virtually meaningless.

Reporter: What has been the most exciting project you have worked on to date?

Scientist: That would be my last project. I had given up all hope of succeeding, and my funding was to run out within days, when **out of the blue**, new information came to light which greatly influenced my results and ensured that my funding would be renewed.

Reporter: I guess you could say the new information came just **in the nick of time**.

Scientist: Absolutely.

Idiom	Meaning	Real-life Situations
be under pressure		
burn the midnight oil		
roll up one's sleeves and dig in		
figure out		
find out		
out of the blue		
in the nick of time		

FUNCTIONS OF NOUN CLAUSES

Exercise A

Review the different functions of noun clauses on pages 76 and 77 in the Student Book. Underline the noun clauses in the following sentences and state their grammatical function.

1. It's a good thing that governments have strict regulations about how far scientists can go with experiments.

   Function: _____

2. That aliens have visited earth is a completely ludicrous suggestion.

   Function: _____

3. The idea that we can grow human organs is just amazing.

   Function: _____

4. The theory is that we will be making regular trips to other planets in the near future.

   Function: _____

5. It seems likely that scientists will try to grow a human heart in the future.

   Function: _____

6. An official inquiry will look into who was responsible for the mix-up.

   Function: _____

7. Sahib was doubtful that his view of the future would be shared by others.

   Function: _____

Grammar in Use

Exercise B

Complete the following sentences by providing noun clause subjects.

EXAMPLE: _____ is a mystery to us.

   Whether there is life on other planets is a mystery to us.

1. _____ worries me.

2. _____ is of concern to everyone.

3. _____ supports the notion that researchers will soon be able to grow other human organs.

4. _____ demonstrates that many people are uncomfortable with stem cell research.

5. _____ is a huge problem.

6. _____ is not universally accepted.

Exercise C

The following descriptions outline some technological developments. Record your thoughts about the developments in a sentence using the following structure: **The fact/idea/news/discovery + "that" noun clause.**

EXAMPLE: The Canadarm is a large Canadian-made robotic arm which allows astronauts on space missions to do repairs.

   The fact that an important part of the International Space Station is Canadian shows the cooperation between countries.

1. The Internet initially had limited use, with the military and academic institutions being the main users. Since it has been made accessible to the public, it has enabled millions to have information at their fingertips. Regulating this electronic medium remains a challenge for police who attempt to track down cyberspace criminals.

   _____

   _____

2. The original computer filled an entire room. Approximately 35 years later, this monster had been replaced by a machine able to sit on a desktop. Only 10 years after that, the computer was reduced to the size of a laptop. Today, the size, convenience, and affordability of the computer have made it an integral part of our daily lives. If the current trend continues, all of us will have hand-held computers in the near future.

   _____

   _____

3. Cars that burn fossil fuels continue to pollute our air. Scientists have been experimenting unsuccessfully with electric cars. As yet, they have not found a way to make them cheap and powerful. Now they are trying to use hydrogen fuel cells to power cars. These fuel cells work by combining hydrogen and oxygen. The hydrogen can be obtained from water, natural gas, or municipal waste, using electricity or heat. This type of fuel production would have no impact on the environment. The challenge is to make the engines much cheaper than the several thousands of dollars they currently cost. Perhaps within the decade we will be driving environmentally friendly cars.

   _____

   _____

4. Studies of DNA have allowed scientists to identify the genes responsible for deadly diseases and, in some cases, repair these genes. In the near future, researchers hope to be able to recode defective genes in order to make them start working correctly. This would allow for the reversal of terminal diseases like cancer.

_____

_____

5. Virtual reality is a powerful technology. It is currently being used to train pilots using simulated flights that are incredibly realistic. Doctors have been able to use 3-D images from CAT scans to virtually recreate a person's insides, thus locating problems more quickly and more easily than with traditional X-rays. Helmets and goggles have been developed to enable the wearer to enter a virtual world and take "totally virtual" vacations.

_____

_____

Exercise D

Complete the following sentences using noun clauses as objects of the prepositions.

EXAMPLE: Everyone has heard **about**...

Everyone has heard about <u>what scientists hope to achieve with stem cell research.</u>

1. I am especially interested **in** _____

_____

_____

2. Do you honestly approve **of** _____

_____

_____

3. The studies focus **on** _____

_____

_____

4. In the future, scientists will look **at** _____

_____

_____

5. People cannot rely **on** _____

_____

_____

6. Do you agree **with** _____

_____

_____

Exercise E
Editing

Scientists recently announced that they have successfully recreated human organs from stem cells. Many people were concerned about the possible implications of this success. The following sentences discuss this topic. Note that the sentences contain errors in their use of noun clauses. Underline these errors and write the correct form above the error.

1. People asked why wanted the scientists to do this type of experiment.

2. The scientists indicated them that they hoped to use stem cells to reverse diseases.

3. The people asked if they had considered the possible negative implications to the scientists.

4. According to the scientists, it was important that be done this type of research despite the possible negative implications.

5. The people told the scientists that would like to see experiments with stem cells taken from human embryos stopped immediately.

6. What would that do is prevent scientists from further developing their understanding of the power of stem cells.

7. Working together, the people and scientists discussed how could they continue research in a way that does not involve stem cells taken from embryos.

Vocabulary 2

Exercise A

astro	dynam	graph
bio	geo	path
cyclo		

Build as many words as you can from each root word by combining each root word with one or more word parts. Use a separate sheet of paper.

asty	logical	nomy
auto	logist	ogen
centric	logy	o
chemistry	mat	para
cracy	mation	photo
crat	meter	physics
degradable	metry	politics
ic	mobile	psy
ism	naut	rhythm
litho	ne	tele

EXAMPLE: bio + degradable = biodegradable

tele + graph = telegraph

One Step Beyond—Create an Activity

Exercise B

From the list you created in Exercise A, select ten words that you are unfamiliar with. Look up their meanings in the dictionary. Write definitions for them in your own words. Exchange these definitions with a partner and try to identify which words are being defined.

Writing

The Expository Paragraph

The expository paragraph explains or analyzes an idea. The writer uses specific details and examples to support his or her value judgment or opinion about the topic. An anecdote or other personal illustration can also be used to support the topic sentence. Expository writing is very common in scientific and medical fields.

An effective expository paragraph

- explains or analyzes an idea.
- indicates the attitude of the writer towards the subject.
- is arranged in a logical order (generally order of importance, order of familiarity, or chronological order).
- includes only those aspects and details that support the controlling idea in the topic sentence.
- provides examples that accurately illustrate the main points.
- sufficiently explains examples to show how they support the controlling idea in the topic sentence.
- uses transitional expressions (such as *another example*, *to illustrate*, *for instance*, *to begin with*, *furthermore*, and *in addition*) to link the examples.

Exercise A

Write topic sentences for the following outlines.

Outline 1

1. At a large car manufacturing plant, automation has eliminated the need for thousands of workers.
2. At the utility companies, work staff was reduced with the introduction of computer-controlled processes.
3. Small offices have been able to reduce staff by increasing their use of office automation.

Outline 2

1. Elizabeth has always supported AIDS research.
2. Jennifer has lent her support to AIDS fundraising.
3. Heather helps out regularly at AIDS hospices.

Exercise B

Circle the controlling idea in the following topic sentences. Write examples of an anecdote or other illustration to support each sentence.

1. Advances in technology have enabled us to explore places where no human has visited.

   _____

   _____

2. Gene manipulation has gone too far.

   _____

   _____

3. Star Trek has had many successful spin-offs.

   _____

   _____

Exercise C

In the following paragraph, identify the following:

1. the topic sentence
2. the controlling idea
3. the way the examples are sequenced (by importance, by time, by familiarity).
4. the examples that support the controlling idea (underline these)

Hollywood has produced several science-fiction movies, now considered classics, that have given us possible glimpses of our future. *Metropolis,* released in 1927, portrayed a future where humans were divided into two distinct groups, the thinkers who envision the goals but can't make them happen and the workers, who can make the plans work but don't have any vision. In 1968, MGM released *2001: A Space Odyssey*. The movie depicted man's epic space journey to discover the alien source that had been supporting mankind's evolution. It ended with a classic struggle of man versus machine, where man emerged superior. Space travel to distant planets was once again an integral part of a movie when *Star Wars* hit the big screen. In 1977, Luke Skywalker jetted across the universe in an attempt to rescue Princess Leia and destroy the Death Star, a horrifying weapon capable of annihilating entire worlds. The movie gave viewers visions of other galaxies and their inhabitants. Futuristic worlds controlled by computers took on a new twist with *The Matrix,* which was released in 1999. It was the first of a trilogy which depicted humans' struggle to seek freedom from the fake world that the machine-made android-like humans had created. Considering the billions that these classics have generated and the continued growth of loyal fans, Hollywood is sure to keep pumping out great sci-fi movies.

Exercise D
Editing

The following outlines contain sentences with structural problems. In addition, there are flaws in the sequencing of the examples. Rewrite the outlines, rearranging the supporting examples so that they follow a logical sequence, and then correct the sentences with structural problems.

Outline 1

Topic Sentence:	Downsizing in companies as a result in technological advances has had a tremendous personal impact about workers.
Example:	It's been documented about that men who lose their jobs sometimes have serious problems with their families.
Example:	It's the idea that they no longer useful are that leads some men into personal depression.
Example:	It is a fact that many men have been in their late fifties who laid off have been unable to rejoin the workforce and consequently are losing everything they had ever.

Outline 2

Topic Sentence:	Advances in technological have created increasingly destructive weapons of war.
Example:	The fact about that guns enabled soldiers to kill at greatly distances increased the bloodshed conflicts incredibly.
Example:	That soldiers when could only kill when at arm's length from each other had limited casualties to some extent.
Example:	The fact that nuclear bombs annihilate can instantly everything within a wide radius of landing has brought unlimited killing capacity from war.

Exercise E

Using one of the outlines in Exercise D, write a paragraph. You will have to further clarify the examples and provide transitions.

Exercise F

Write an expository paragraph about one of the following topics. Start with an outline. Use the Expository Paragraph Checklist below to edit your work.

1. Bionic body parts
2. Impact of science fiction
3. Human organ growth
4. Technological developments

☑ Expository Paragraph Checklist

- ☐ Have I considered my audience and purpose?
- ☐ Have I narrowed my topic?
- ☐ Does my topic sentence indicate what will be explained and what my attitude or opinion towards it is? (controlling idea)
- ☐ Have I organized my paragraph logically with my examples presented in their order of importance, order of familiarity, or time order?
- ☐ Have I ensured that all the examples are sufficiently explained and that the link to the controlling idea is clear?
- ☐ Have I used transitional expressions adequately and appropriately?
- ☐ Have I checked my paragraph to make sure the meaning of each sentence is clear?
- ☐ Have I checked my paragraph to make sure that I have used precise words and the correct forms of the words?
- ☐ Have I proofread my paragraph for errors in grammar, punctuation, and spelling?

Academic Word List

computer	despite	minorities
concept	economic	normal
constraints	evidence	phase
construction	evolution	philosophy
contribution	granted	role
create	link	transfer
credit	medical	

Exercise A
Word Meaning

Circle the word in parentheses that matches each of the following definitions.

1. the activity of building something (computation / conception / construction)
2. something given to produce or achieve something (constrain / contribution / recreate)
3. to join (design / link / transfer)
4. as usual; the regular way (creative / evidence / normal)
5. to invent something (transfer / link / create)
6. praise or recognition (grant / role / credit)
7. a function or position (phase / role / concept)
8. a limitation or constriction (constraint / design / economy)
9. to move from one place to another (link / create / transfer)
10. related to money, trade, or industry (economic / contribution / philosophy)
11. a gradual process of change and development (contribution / construction / evolution)
12. a machine used for storing and processing data (computer / phase / role)
13. a stage in a process of development (design / phase / evolution)
14. related to the treatment of an illness or injury (medical / computer / normal)
15. a particular set of beliefs, values and principles (contribution / philosophy / normal)
16. a reason to believe something is true (evidence / normal / concept)
17. an idea or principle (design / phase / concept)
18. not prevented by (link / despite / phase)
19. to accept as true (grant / design / transfer)
20. small groups in society that are different from the rest (contribution / minorities / phase)

Exercise B
Pronunciation—Syllables & Stress

Listen to your teacher or an audio dictionary to hear the pronunciation for each word in the list. Repeat each word aloud. Mark the syllables and major word stress.

1. computer (n): com / **pŭt** / er
2. concept (n): _____
3. constraints (n): _____
4. construction (n): _____
5. contribution (n): _____
6. create (v): _____
7. credit (v): _____
8. despite (prep): _____
9. economic (adj): _____
10. evidence (n): _____

11. evolution (n): _____

12. granted (v): _____

13 link (n): _____

14. medical (adj): _____

15. minorities (n): _____

16. normal (adj): _____

17. phase (n): _____

18. philosophy (n): _____

19. role (n): _____

20 transfer (v): _____

Exercise C
Word Forms

Fill in each blank with the word form indicated in parentheses. More than one word may be possible for each indicated word form.

1. computer (n): _____ (v)
   _____ (adj)

2. concept (n): _____ (v)
   _____ (adj) _____ (adv)

3. constraints (n): _____ (v)
   _____ (adj)

4. construction (n): _____ (v)
   _____ (adj)

5. contribution (n): _____ (v)

6. create (v): _____ (n)
   _____ (adj) _____ (adv)

7. credit (v): _____ (n)

8. economic (adj): _____ (n)
   _____ (adv)

9. evidence (n): _____ (adj)

10. evolution (n): _____ (v)

11. granted (v): _____ (n)

12. link (n): _____ (adj)

13. minorities (n): _____ (adj)

14. medical (adj): _____ (n)

15. normal (adj): _____ (adv)

16. philosophy (n): _____ (v)
    _____ (adj) _____ (adv)

17. transfer (v): _____ (adj)

Exercise D

In a dictionary, find one example sentence for each circled word in Exercise A; copy it into your notebook. Draft a second sentence of your own. Then, work with a partner to revise and edit your sentence.

Exercise E

Read the following story and complete each blank with one of the words from the list. You do not have to change the grammatical form of any of the words. Use each word only once.

constraints	economic	minor
contributions	evidence	normal
created	grants	reconstruct
despite	medical	role

Scientists have played a critical $_1$ _____ in restoring a reasonably $_2$ _____ quality of life for victims of severe accidents. Funded by government $_3$ _____ which they have applied for and received, scientists have $_4$ _____ artificial body parts that can be used to $_5$ _____ missing or damaged limbs. $_6$ _____ certain $_7$ _____ such as the high cost of bionic body parts, there is ample $_8$ _____ to suggest that the $_9$ _____ the recipients can make to society outweigh the $_{10}$ _____ strain on the $_{11}$ _____ system which is $_{12}$ _____ when compared to the long-term health care costs of people who are not mobile.

computers	evolved	philosophy
concept	link	transfer
credited	phase	

Do you know who is $_{13}$ _____ with conceptualizing the latest envelope-thin design of the new Mac $_{14}$ _____? The $_{15}$ _____ of designing a computer so thin it can fit in an envelope is amazing. Its light weight and high portability has certainly $_{16}$ _____from the computers of the 70s that could fill an entire room. The ultra-thin computer really is the next $_{17}$ _____ of computer design. You can now $_{18}$ _____ to the Internet and $_{19}$ _____ your files to another computer from virtually anywhere in the world. My $_{20}$ _____ about computers is that they can never be too small or too powerful.

Unit 6
It Stands to Reason

Vocabulary 1

Exercise A

Seven words are used in inappropriate grammatical forms in the reading below. Find the words, cross them out, and write in their appropriate forms above the crossed out words.

Logic is a form of thinking that is valued in many cultures. The ability to reasonable is developed from very early on. As early as kindergarten, children learn to draw conclude from facts, to categorize information
5 into logical groupings, and to understand analog. The classic math problems learned in grade school, that we thought tested the ability to do sums, were really designed to develop the ability to reason. "If Johnny buys half as many eggs as his brother, and his brother
10 buys six dozen, how many eggs does Johnny buy?" This might seem like a simple math problem, but it is the first step in learning how to interpret facts in order to draw logical conclusions.

Grouping information into logically categories is not
15 only useful in developing reasoning skills but also in learning how to write in English. We love categories. Anyone who learns how to write an English essay will learn how to categorize information in both the planning and writing of the essay. As children, we were
20 drilled in exercises asking us "Which item doesn't fit?" Look at the pictures of the raincoat, the umbrella, the rain boots, and the sandals—which one doesn't belong?

When we were asked these questions, we were learning how to group items, ideas, and thoughts.
25 These activities were really precursors to writing. Activities in which we had to look for similarities, and then relate them to other similarities, were abundant. In the beginning, it was "what two items are alike?" but we quickly moved to "eye is to eyelid as window is to
30 _____." These were not designed just as fun word games; they developed our abilities to understand relationships—a thinking skill that becomes critical in solving problems in our daily lives.

Of course, as we got older we were exposed to prob-
35 lems that required more creative solutions. "The city council is trying to battle youth crime in a neighbourhood known for its high unemployment and drug problem. What can the community do?" Finding solutions to these types of problems requires critical-thinking skills and the
40 wise that comes with experience. Emphasizing rational argue and objective thinking is deemed as essential in North American culture as it is in much of the world. Biasing thinking may be common, but it is not very useful in our advanced social structure. And if we are to realize
45 our full potentials as thinking human beings, we must continue to exercise our minds through critical thought as we exercise our bodies through physical activities—but that's an analogy that just stands to reason.

Exercise B

Find definitions for the following words and then fill in the blanks with the correct grammatical form of the words.

analogy	knowledge	spatial
argument	opinion	wisdom
bias	puzzle	

1. Clear-cutting forests is _____ to destroying the planet.

2. The newly-hired MBA* graduate was very _____ about her subject specialty, but she lacked the interpersonal skills to do the job well.

3. We will never solve the world's environmental problems until we address world hunger and poverty. What is your _____?

4. No matter how much you know, _____ only comes with experience.

5. Reporters are supposed to be objective and not show political _____.

6. Cartographers must have well-developed _____ intelligence to design maps.

7. Because of the weak _____ he presented, the speaker was unable to convince his audience that child labour is a serious problem.

8. The detective was _____ by the conflicting evidence in the murder case.

* MBA (Masters of Business Administration): in North America, an advanced degree in business.

Grammar Focus 1

"IF" STATEMENTS (CONDITIONALS)

Exercise A

Match the sentence parts from Column A to those in Column B.

Column A	Column B
1. If the school year were extended,	a) teachers wouldn't have needed to spend so much time reviewing last year's material.
2. If more emphasis were placed on learning how to learn,	b) students are more likely to be successful later in life.
3. If you really want to learn a second language,	c) students will not forget what they've learned so easily.
4. If the school year had been extended,	d) immerse yourself in it.
5. If more emphasis had been placed on learning how to learn,	e) students would find continuous learning more agreeable.
6. If more emphasis is placed on learning how to learn,	f) you would study it in school.
7. If you really wanted to learn a second language,	g) students would not necessarily learn more.
8. If the school year is extended,	h) the employees would have found it easier to adapt to the technological changes in the workplace.

Exercise B

Some of the following sentences are grammatically correct, others are incorrect. Mark whether the sentence is correct (C) or incorrect (I). Then correct the incorrect sentences.

☐ 1. I would not have made some of those mistakes if I thought more critically.

☐ 2. You are less likely to be able to solve complex problems if you do not consider multiple viewpoints.

☐ 3. If the parents provided a more stimulating environment for the infant, his intellect would have developed more.

☐ 4. Students learn English better if they will read a variety of materials.

☐ 5. You can learn almost anything if you are motivated.

☐ 6. If you read newspapers every day, you would have been much smarter.

☐ 7. If she believed that learning increases your enjoyment of life, she would make more of an effort to learn.

Exercise C

Read the facts presented in the following sentences. Then create new sentences that suggest how the situation could be changed.

EXAMPLE: *Fact*: Jeremy didn't study for the test, so he didn't do well.

Response: If Jeremy *had studied* for the test, he *would have done* better.

EXAMPLE: *Fact*: The student registered at this college, but he is not sure whether he was given a student identification (ID) number.

Response: If the student *registered* at this college, (then) the student *was given* a student identification number.

EXAMPLE: *Fact*: I don't know the answer; that's why I'm not telling you.

Response: If I *knew* the answer, I *would tell* you.

EXAMPLE: *Fact*: You didn't finish high school. Your chances of finding a job now are not good.

Response: If you *had finished* high school, you *would have* a better chance of finding a job now.

1. Randa values education so she studies hard.

_____

_____

2. As a young man, Peter was interested in science, so he became an engineer.

_____

_____

3. Margaret is a teacher, so she knows what will be expected of her children when they get to high school.

_____

_____

4. Cosmo never liked to write, so he didn't write very often.

_____

_____

5. Tina takes her young daughter Chloë to the library every week, so Chloë feels very comfortable there.

_____

_____

6. Chris began piano lessons at the age of four, so now at the age of six he already plays quite well.

_____

_____

7. Nicholas is very interested in science, so his mother sent him to science camp in the summer.

_____

_____

8. Young Martin spends a lot of time with his Spanish-speaking grandparents, so he speaks Spanish as well as English.

_____

_____

Grammar in Use
Exercise D

Education reform is popular in many countries of the world. What changes could be made to the education system in your country of origin, and what consequences would these changes have? Write ten sentences that state your point of view.

EXAMPLE: If students were given more homework in my country, they would learn better study habits.

Vocabulary 2

Exercise A

Phrasal Verbs

Fill in the blanks with a form of the appropriate phrasal verb.

focus on
figure out
account for
work towards
bring about
find out

Memorandum

To: Kerry Powers
From: Lisa Montgomery
Date: January 5, 2009

Re: Production Meeting

In Tuesday's initial production meeting, I would like to 1 _____ the following agenda items:

1. Scope of the Advanced English Course program
2. Skeletal outline of program contents
3. Project workback schedule

Although we have already discussed the scope of this project with the authors in general terms, I would like to clarify our objectives at this meeting. We will have to 2 _____ what the essential content should be, so please think about this before the meeting. Also, 3 _____ what the authors plan to include in the program before the meeting. This will not only facilitate our discussions, but ensure that we're 4 _____ a common goal.

You mentioned that you anticipate expenditures beyond those 5 _____ in the original project budget. You will need to present some good arguments if you want to 6 _____ a change in the budget. Prepare a memo, addressed to me, outlining what additional expenses you anticipate. Explain why these expenses are necessary and what the resulting benefits will be.

Kerry, I look forward to working with you on this project and I'm certain we will once again produce an excellent product.

Exercise B

When a verb combines with an adverb or a preposition to create a new meaning, it is called a phrasal verb. List as many meanings as possible for the individual verbs listed below, and then write definitions for the phrasal verbs.

1. to focus: _____

   to focus on: _____

2. to figure: _____

   to figure out: _____

3. to account: _____

   to account for: _____

4. to work: _____

   to work towards: _____

5. to bring: _____

   to bring about: _____

6. to find: _____

   to find out: _____

One Step Beyond—Create an Activity

Exercise C

Write sentences using each individual verb and each phrasal verb in Exercise B. Rewrite the sentences leaving out the target phrasal verb or individual verbs. Exchange your work with a classmate and complete the activity you receive.

Grammar Focus 2

MODALS

Exercise A

The president has been murdered. He was stabbed 20 times. The following bar line shows how probable each fact is. Write sentences of deduction for each fact, using modals of probability.

Yes 100%

a) 95%   yes—the victim screamed
b) 75%   yes—the cook killed him
c) 50%   yes/no—the maid saw the murderer
d) 75%   no—the wife killed him (she claims to have an alibi)

No 100%

e) 100% no—the president committed suicide

Grammar Expansion

"If" Statements with Modals

Conditional sentences can also be expressed with modals. In conditional sentences, modals are used in the same way as in other sentences. The rules about tenses in conditional sentences still apply.

EXAMPLES: *(possible condition / unspecified time)*

(deduced result / unspecified time)

If Lisa is a good critical thinker, she *must* be good at solving complex problems.

(real past condition) *(deduced past result)*

If no one *could* understand the explanation, it *must* have been too complicated.

Exercise B

Add words to create sentences that show a condition-and-result relationship. You may have to change the order of phrases.

1. study hard / have to / do well on test

   _____

2. know one foreign language / should / easier to learn another

   _____

3. write the summary / not read the book / be able to

   _____

4. suspect / can't / alibi / committed murder

   _____

5. know something about Middle Eastern history / might / understand context of the president's speech

   _____

Exercise C

Read the following excerpt on problem-solving from a college-level psychology text and then answer the questions that follow on a separate sheet.

Becoming Better at Problem-solving

The first step in successfully solving a problem is to interpret or represent the problem correctly. You can then experiment with a number of solution strategies, shifting your perspective on the problem from one angle to another. Let's look more closely at how some of these strategies work.

Tactic of elimination

If in solving a given problem you are more sure of what you do not want than of what you do want, the **tactic of elimination** can be very helpful. The best approach is first to create a list of all the possible solutions you can think of. Then discard all the solutions that take you where you definitely do not want to go. That leaves a smaller number of potential solutions for you to examine much more closely. This strategy will only work if your list of possible solutions contains at least one good solution to the problem. Otherwise, you'll end up eliminating all the possible solutions on your list, and you'll have to start all over again from scratch! Also, you have to be careful not to scrap a solution that *seems* on the surface to lead to an undesirable outcome, but on closer examination, might turn out to be an excellent solution to the problem.

Visualizing

Other useful tactics include **visualizing**, diagramming, and charting various courses of action. By drawing a diagram of a problem, or even constructing a simple model of it, you may find it easier to grasp the principle of the problem and to avoid irrelevant or distracting details. Some chess masters, for example, can visualize chess games in their heads; as a result, they are able to play as many as 50 simultaneous games blindfolded!

Creative problem-solving

Many problems, of course, do not lend themselves to straightforward solutions but rely more on flexible and original thinking. For example, how many unusual uses can you think of for an ordinary object like a brick? It's easy to imagine a few good uses for a brick but quite another task to come up with 50 or 60 distinct uses.

Psychologists sometimes refer to this type of thinking as **divergent thinking**, as opposed to **convergent thinking**. A problem requiring convergent thinking has only one or a very few solutions—like a math problem. Convergent thinking is required when a problem has a known solution. By contrast, problems that have no single correct solution and that require a flexible, inventive approach, call for divergent thinking.

Because creative problem-solving requires thinking up new and original ideas, the process is not always aided by planning or the deliberate use of problem-solving strategies. Solutions to many problems rely on insight, a seemingly arbitrary flash "out of the blue" that reveals the solution to a problem. Therefore, if you simply cannot arrive at a solution to a problem after careful preparation and step-by-step efforts at problem-solving, it might be wise to stop thinking about the problem for a while and return to it later, approaching it from a new angle. Sometimes you get so enmeshed in the details of a problem that you lose sight of an obvious solution. Taking a rest from the problem may allow a fresh approach to surface.

It is also important to develop a questioning attitude toward problems. Ask yourself, "What is the real problem here? Can the problem be interpreted in other ways?" By *redefining* the problem, you may find that you have opened up new avenues to creative solutions. And try to maintain an uncritical attitude toward potential solutions: Don't reject a prospective solution because at first glance it doesn't seem to fit that problem. On closer examination, the solution may turn out to be highly effective, or it may bring to mind similar solutions that would work. This is the rationale behind the technique called **brainstorming**—when solving a problem, produce lots of ideas without evaluating them prematurely. Only after lots of ideas have been collected should you review and evaluate them.

Finally, people may become more creative when they interact with creative peers and teachers who serve as role models. Although some creative people work well in isolation, many others find it stimulating to collaborate with other creative people.

1. What should you do as a first step if you are trying to solve a problem?

2. The reading states that the "tactic of elimination" strategy will only work if one condition is met. What is the condition?

3. If the "tactic of elimination" strategy is not suitable for solving a problem, what other strategies can you use?

4. What does the reading suggest you should do if you cannot find a solution to a problem after careful preparation and step-by-step efforts?

5. What may happen if you reject a prospective solution at first glance?

Exercise D

What conclusions or expectations are logical based on the following facts? Be careful. Some facts lead to different degrees of certainty; let the meanings guide you.

EXAMPLES: a) All brothers are male.
b) I have a brother.

If all brothers are male, and I have a brother, my brother must be male.

a) Linda told me she was going to the party.
b) No women are at the party yet.

If no women are at the party yet, Linda is not at the party.

1. a) All carnivores eat meat.
b) My pet is a carnivore.

_____

_____

2. a) Polar bears are white.
b) This bear lives at the North Pole.

_____

_____

3. a) Henry lost his dog, which answers to the name Fado.
b) Jeannie found a dog, which answers to the name Fado.

_____

_____

4. a) Martin's grandparents speak only Spanish.
b) Martin spends a lot of time with his grandparents.

_____

_____

5. a) I have no brothers.
b) Pat is my sibling.

_____

_____

6. a) Paula does not read science-fiction novels.
b) She is reading a novel now.

_____

_____

7. a) The teacher received an essay from an unidentified student about the ethics of genetic engineering.
b) Only two students in the class wrote an essay on this topic.
c) John wrote an essay on the illegal organ transplants.
d) Each student wrote only one essay.

_____

_____

8. a) Anita's mother is Francophone.
b) Anita has lived in English-speaking Edmonton all her life
c) Anita speaks English and French.

_____

_____

One Step Beyond—Create an Activity

Exercise E

Create an activity like the one in Exercise D. Write eight sets of facts and exchange your facts with a classmate. Write *if/then* statements to draw logical conclusions from your classmate's facts.

Vocabulary Expansion

Expressing Cause and Effect
Exercise A

As you read this paragraph about the sources of stress, underline at least five different words or phrases that signal cause or effect. Write the words under the headings that follow the reading.

The first step in learning to manage stress is to understand its causes. It is important to understand that stress has two defining characteristics: it is a state of tension or a feeling of threat and it requires us to
5 change or adapt. The most common source of stress is change. People prefer continuity and predictability in their lives. But change by itself isn't necessarily stressful. Consider the example of driving on a road and coming to a red light. We have to change our behaviour and stop. Stopping at the red light, however, does
10

not necessarily lead to stress. If, on the other hand, we are late for an appointment, having to stop at the red light may indeed result in stress. Stress may also result from pressure. When we feel forced to speed up, inten-
15 sify, or achieve a higher standard of performance, we experience pressure. Sometimes, pressure is internally imposed, as in the case of personal standards of excellence. Other times, it results from external sources, such as the media or our peers; many people feel pres-
20 sured by the need to conform to the social standards of beauty modelled on television and in magazines. A third source of stress is frustration. This is the feeling we experience when we are prevented from reaching a goal because something or someone stands in our way.
25 The worker who is bypassed for a promotion because of discriminatory practices experiences frustration. Once we understand the causes of stress, we can begin to work on managing, and possibly reducing, it.

Words that signal cause	Words that signal effect
_____	_____
_____	_____
_____	_____
_____	_____
_____	_____
_____	_____
_____	_____

Add other words or phrases you know that can signal cause or effect. Use a thesaurus to help you.

Exercise B

Write sentences to express the following cause and effect relationships. Use the words and phrases you identified in Exercise A.

1. prolong life / fear death

_____

_____

2. high self-esteem / parental praise and feeling secure

_____

_____

3. smoking / cancer

_____

_____

4. infant stimulation / increase intelligence

_____

_____

5. ability to reason / exercising the mind

_____

_____

6. academic performance / nutrition and sleep

_____

_____

7. lack of exercise / poor health

_____

_____

8. criminal activity / high unemployment

_____

_____

9. relationships suffer / poor communication

_____

_____

10. explosion / gas leak

_____

_____

Writing

Cause and Effect Paragraphs

It is impossible to go through a single day in our lives without either consciously or subconsciously analyzing the causes and effects of our actions, and those of everything around us.

In the cause and effect paragraph, a writer seeks to understand a topic by analyzing it. When causes are analyzed, the writer attempts to understand why a certain event occurred. When effects are analyzed, the writer considers the results of a certain event. Based on the findings, the reader may also be able to predict results or effects, given similar circumstances. Because of the shortness of a paragraph, the writer would normally address either the cause or the effect, but not both. The paragraph is generally organized according to familiarity or interest when the causes or effects are of equal significance. If some causes or effects are obviously more important than some of the others, the factors should be presented from most important to least important.

This type of writing is very common among professionals dealing with individuals, such as doctors, nurses, teachers, supervisors, and psychologists.

Cause and effect paragraphs can be evaluative, where the writer indicates his or her own opinions about the cause or effect. This type of writing forces the writer to judge the information and form an opinion. The paragraph can also be informative, where the writer merely presents the facts, trying to keep the paragraph as objective as possible.

An effective cause and effect paragraph
- analyzes either the causes or the results of a particular event.
- is arranged in a logical order (generally order of importance, order of familiarity, or time order).
- has a topic sentence that briefly states the causes or effects to be examined (if it is an informative paragraph), or has a controlling idea that states the writer's feelings towards the event (if it is an evaluative paragraph).
- includes sufficient detail to explain the cause or effect of a particular event.
- uses transitional expressions to link the causes or effects.

Exercise A

Work individually or in teams. List at least five possible **causes** of each of the following topics.

1. high unemployment
2. high crime
3. poverty

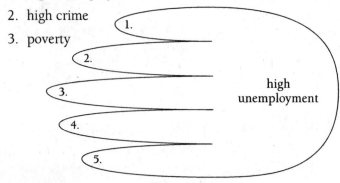

Now list at least five possible **results** of each of the following topics.

1. constant criticism
2. slackening of academic standards
3. racial prejudice

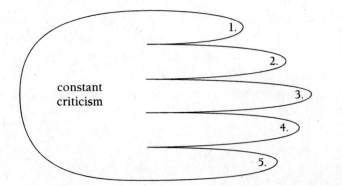

Exercise B

In order to convince the reader that the opinion or idea you expressed in a topic sentence is valid (true), you must support your ideas. You can support an idea with examples, anecdotes, statistics, definitions, or reasoning. You will have to choose what works best.

For each of the following topics, agree with one of the opinions and write three ideas that support your position.

1. The effects of parental expectations on children
   a) Parents must continually set high expectations for their children if the children are to achieve success.
   b) When parents continually set high expectations for their children, they send their children a message that a person's worth is measured by achievements, rather than by the type of person he or she is.

   _____

   _____

2. Many young children today are having difficulty learning to spell
   a) There is no proven correlation between the amount of television a young child watches and the difficulty he or she has learning to spell.
   b) Many young children today are having difficulty learning to spell because of poor reading habits.

   _____

   _____

3. The results of encouraging competition in children
   a) Encouraging children to be competitive in sports, in academics, and in their personal relationships discourages them from sharing and cooperating with others, and sets them up for failure in a workforce that values teamwork.
   b) Encouraging children to be competitive in sports, in academics, and in their personal relationships encourages self-discipline and goal-setting, and prepares them for the world of work.

   _____

   _____

Exercise C
Editing

Edit the following paragraph for errors in grammar and punctuation.

If I teach my children only one skill, it would be to learn how to learn. In our fast-changing technological society, if one can't learn new skills quickly and adapt to new ideas, one was lost. Gone are the days when rote learning led the way to knowledge and success. As little as 50 years ago, if you are knowledgeable you are admired. If you had a college or university degree, you were guaranteed a good job. If knowledge will be all you can offer an employer today, you're not worth hiring; today's knowledge is obsolete tomorrow. However, if you had known where and how to access knowledge you have a transferable skill that will never become obsolete. If you can understood how you, as an individual, learn best and can acquire the skills for learning, your road will have been paved with opportunity. If, on the other hand, you focus only on what you are learning, without ever understanding the process, each new learning experience may have lead to frustration and possibly failure.

Exercise D

Complete these writing activities. Use the Cause and Effect Paragraph Checklist to edit your work.

1. Design a brochure for a private English-language school. Include a paragraph that explains the benefits of learning English as a second language.

2. Write a speech for students who are about to enter high school. Discuss the causes of failing to achieve academic success in high school and the importance of becoming a successful learner.

3. Write a sales letter soliciting business for a new fitness club and health centre. Include a paragraph about the benefits of a healthy lifestyle.

☑ Cause and Effect Paragraph Checklist

☐ Have I considered my audience and purpose?

☐ Have I narrowed my topic?

☐ Does my topic sentence indicate if I will be discussing causes or effects?

☐ Have I supported my opinion if my paragraph is evaluative (opinion)?

☐ Have I provided enough information if my paragraph is informative (fact)?

☐ Have I organized my paragraph logically, with my examples presented in their order of familiarity, interest, or importance?

☐ Have I used transitional expressions adequately and appropriately?

☐ Have I ensured that all the causes or effects are sufficiently explained and that their link to the topic sentence is clear?

☐ Have I checked my paragraph to make sure the meaning of each sentence is clear?

☐ Have I checked my paragraph to make sure that I have used precise words and the correct form of words?

☐ Have I proofread my paragraph for errors in grammar, punctuation, and spelling?

Academic Word List

adjustment	immigration	response
approximated	legal	specific
assume	logic	statistics
authority	maintenance	strategies
context	promote	sufficient
deduction	published	survey
goals	relevant	

Exercise A
Word Meaning

Circle the word in parentheses that matches each of the following definitions.

1. In order to make good decisions, you must have information that is <u>relevant</u>.
   a) happened within the last five years
   b) connected with the topic
   c) interesting to the decision maker

2. Some people argue that Canada needs immigrants in order to grow and <u>maintain</u> a good economy.
   a) continue having
   b) have in the future
   c) had in the past

3. Logical thinking is necessary but not <u>sufficient</u> for thinking critically. One must also have good information, distinguish between factions and opinions, and consider biases and multiple points of view.
   a) desirable
   b) hopeful
   c) enough

4. We should not <u>assume</u> that information on the Internet is reliable.
   a) accept that something is true without proof
   b) reject something without proof
   c) find out if something is true

5. In a good argument, the speaker should be able to provide <u>specific</u> examples for claims, rather than speak in general terms.
   a) many
   b) definite
   c) other

6. Opinions can be supported by anecdotes, <u>statistics</u>, and examples.
   a) the mathematics of probability
   b) the science of logic
   c) people's intuition

7. A good thinker will adjust his or her <u>conclusions</u> as new information arises.
   a) questions about a topic
   b) opinions that are based on emotion
   c) decisions based on evidence and reasoning

8. What can you <u>deduce</u> from these particular pieces of information that might lead to a general conclusion?
   a) decide based on evidence and logic
   b) ask based on new information
   c) guess based on your own opinions

9. Information based on research is more <u>authoritative</u> than information based on personal experience.
   a) unreliable
   b) complete and accurate
   c) open to interpretation

10. In order for a <u>survey</u> to be reliable and valid, the sample size must be large.
    a) a research method that asks people questions
    b) an Internet site with a lot of information
    c) a conclusion based on one person's opinion

11. The activities of the government may be <u>legal</u>, yet not be ethical.
    a) in agreement with religious beliefs
    b) in agreement with the people's wishes
    c) in agreement with the law

12. One <u>strategy</u> for solving complex problems is to explore the causes and consequences of the problems.
    a) a past experience that was not successful
    b) a detailed plan for achieving success in something
    c) a wrong guess about what the problem is

13. His <u>response</u> to the information was subjective. It was not based on reason, but on personal emotions.
    a) reaction
    b) question
    c) opinion

14. Teachers often engage their students in classroom debates to <u>promote</u> critical thinking.
    a) reject
    b) encourage
    c) give the opposite point of view

15. The preliminary survey results were just an <u>approximation.</u> The detailed results will be reported after careful analysis of the data.
    a) calculation based on chance
    b) amount most people disagree with
    c) estimate

16. It is important to understand a problem in its <u>context</u>.
    a) individual parts, rather than the whole
    b) the situation in which something happens
    c) existing as an idea rather than as a real thing

17. The <u>goal</u> of identifying biases is to challenge them.
    a) aim or purpose
    b) source or origins
    c) difficulty or challenge

18. Canada is a multicultural country because of the many <u>immigrants</u> that settle here.
    a) people who move from one country to another country to live there
    b) people who travel a lot
    c) people who study abroad

19. Today, anyone can <u>publish</u> his or her ideas and opinions on the Internet. That's why we have to be careful about trusting the Internet as a source of reliable information.
    a) search for information in the media
    b) argue about other people's ideas
    c) make information available to people

20. Decisions are better when they are based on <u>logic</u> as well as emotions, rather than on emotions alone.
    a) a way of thinking that is based on good judgment
    b) a way of expressing emotions in words
    c) a way of disagreeing with someone

Exercise B
Pronunciation—Syllables and Stress

Listen to your teacher or an audio dictionary to hear the pronunciation for each word in the list. Repeat each word aloud. Mark the syllables and major word stress.

1. adjustment (n): ad / jŭst / ment
2. approximated (v): _____
3. assume (v): _____
4. authority (n): _____
5. context (n): _____
6. deduction (n): _____
7. goals (n): _____
8. immigration (n): _____
9. legal (adj): _____
10. logic (n): _____
11. maintenance (n): _____
12. promote (v): _____
13. published (adj): _____
14. relevant (adj): _____
15. response (n): _____
16. specific (adj): _____

17. statistics (n): _____
18. strategies (n): _____
19. sufficient (adj): _____
20. survey (n): _____

Exercise C
Word Forms

Fill in each blank with the word form indicated in parentheses. More than one word may be possible for each indicated word form.

1. adjustment (n): _____ (v) _____ (adj)
2. approximated (v): _____ (n) _____ (adj)
3. assume (v): _____ (n) _____ (adj)
4. authority (n): _____ (v) _____ (adj) _____ (adv)
5. context (n): _____ (v) _____ (adj)
6. deduction (n): _____ (v) _____ (adj)
7. immigration (n): _____ (v)
8. legal (adj): _____ (v) _____ (n)
9. logic (n): _____ (adj) _____ (adv)
10. maintenance (n): _____ (v) _____ (adj)
11. promote (v): _____ (n) _____ (adj)
12. published (adj): _____ (v) _____ (adj)
13. relevant (adj): _____ (n)
14. response (n): _____ (v) _____ (adj)
15. specific (adj): _____ (v) _____ (n)
16. statistics (n): _____ (adj)
17. strategies (n): _____ (v) _____ (adj) _____ (adv)
18. sufficient (adj): _____ (v) _____ (adv)
19. survey (n): _____ (v) _____ (adj)

Exercise D

In a dictionary, find one example sentence for each circled word in Exercise A and copy it into your notebook. Draft a second sentence of your own. Then, work with a partner to revise and edit your sentence.

Exercise E

Read the following story and complete each blank with one of the words from the list. You do not have to change the grammatical form of any of the words. Use each word only once.

authority	published	sufficient
promoted	relevant	

Critical thinking is $_1$ _____ in college classrooms because it is important to challenge the $_2$ _____ of much of the information we get. We should not take it for granted that the opinions $_3$ _____ in books, in newspapers, and on the Internet are supported by $_4$ _____ and $_5$ _____ information.

adjust	logical	specific
context	responses	statistical

We prefer arguments based on $_6$ _____ thinking, $_7$ _____ information, and $_8$ _____ examples instead of subjective $_9$ _____ and generalities. We understand complex problems in the $_{10}$ _____ in which they occur and $_{11}$ _____ our own understanding of complex issues as new information becomes available.

approximately	goal	maintain
assumption	immigration	strategy
deduce	legal	surveys

Take the issue of $_{12}$ _____ to Canada. According to Statistics Canada $_{13}$ _____, Canada accepts $_{14}$ _____ 250,000 $_{15}$ _____ immigrants each year. The $_{16}$ _____ of Canada's immigration policy is to build and $_{17}$ _____ a good economy. At least, that's the $_{18}$ _____. Immigration is also one $_{19}$ _____ for increasing population growth. Policy makers $_{20}$ _____ that if we expand the number of immigrants that come into Canada, the national population will grow.

Unit 7
All the Rage

Vocabulary 1

Exercise A

Use the words in Vocabulary 1 in the Student Book, page 103, to fill in the blanks in the exercise below.

1. Superheroes, music videos, and action films _appeal_ to audiences worldwide.

2. Hollywood blockbuster films are often _____ with massive advertising and merchandising to persuade the public to see them.

3. It's amazing how many people buy trashy entertainment magazines to quench their thirst for show business _____.

4. Today's Bollywood film _____ enjoy a huge fan base around the world.

5. The current North American _____ for the paranormal explains the success of shows like *Heroes*.

6. Music video artists often set worldwide fashion _____.

7. The Apple computer _____ is recognized around the world.

Now, search for the words and circle them in the word grid provided. The words may be written horizontally, vertically, or diagonally, and can be written forwards or backwards. One example has been done for you.

r	t	i	l	f	k	a	p	k	l	m
t	r	r	d	o	s	l	o	d	i	l
g	i	m	m	i	g	k	s	e	b	h
n	v	o	a	i	t	o	c	p	t	c
h	i	p	n	i	n	r	i	y	c	g
m	a	n	i	a	e	a	k	h	d	i
e	l	a	p	p	e	a	l	l	a	m
r	n	o	e	r	t	r	e	n	d	s

Exercise B

For each of the nouns in the left column, write the grammatical form of the word as indicated in parentheses. Then, write a sentence for each of your words on a separate sheet of paper.

1. idol: _____(v)
2. trivia: _____(adj)
3. craze: _____(adj)
4. appeal: _____(adj)
5. trend: _____(adj)
6. mania: _____(adj)
7. hype: _____(adj)

One Step Beyond—Create an Activity

Exercise C

Design a crossword puzzle for your classmates using eight words from this unit. Incorporate each word into a sentence and leave a blank for the missing word.

EXAMPLE: **Across: 1.** Nintendo created tremendous _____ for its Wii video game console long before it was released. (Answer: hype)

Grammar Focus

ADVERB CLAUSES

Exercise A

In the sentences below, the adverb clauses are introduced by an incorrect subordinator. Replace the underlined subordinator with an appropriate one.

1. <u>Once</u> she had studied drama for many years, she could not get a job as an actress.

2. <u>Whereas</u> the arrival of YouTube on the Internet, independent filmmakers have a better chance of distributing their work.

3. It is possible to become a successful Hollywood actor <u>before</u> you are not that talented.

4. Cellphone sales exploded <u>even though</u> computer and telephone technology were able to be integrated.

5. The fashion trends of India will become more and more popular in the West <u>before</u> Bollywood films are successful.

6. <u>As though</u> J.K. Rowling vows that she will not write any more Harry Potter books, the Harry Potter industry of merchandise and films is likely to continue.

7. Every time the singer sings that song, she has to make it sound <u>while</u> she were singing it for the first time.

8. You won't be able to buy tickets for the concert now <u>while</u> you buy from scalpers. (Scalpers = people who sell tickets on the street outside the theatre) .

9. Helen studied dance <u>as if</u> her sister studied music.

10. Some actors become famous <u>once</u> others remain relatively unknown.

Exercise B

For each pair of sentences below, join the two sentences with an adverb clause subordinator that expresses the meaning indicated in parentheses.

1. She learned how to play the guitar. She picked up the violin and viola easily. (relationship of time)

   _____

   _____

2. The actor stopped his monologue in the middle of the sentence. He may have forgotten his lines. (relationship of manner)

   _____

   _____

3. His parents persuaded him to study music at college. They knew that it would be difficult to make a good living being a musician. (relationship of reason)

   _____

   _____

4. We can visit the art museum tomorrow. I don't know if the museum is open on Sundays. (relationship of condition)

   _____

   _____

5. She got the lead role in the film. She was not a professional actress. (relationship of contrast— unexpected result)

   _____

   _____

6. Leslie set her television to record her favourite soap opera at 3:30 p.m. She thought she might not be home from school in time to watch it. (relationship of condition)

   _____

   _____

7. The parents only watched television at night. Their young children had gone to bed. (relationship of time)

   _____

   _____

8. The dancer was not a professional. He danced like a professional. (relationship of manner)

   _____

   _____

Exercise C

Read the following text about reality television—a world-wide pop culture trend—and then complete the sentences using appropriate adverb clause subordinators.

What is Reality TV?

Reality TV is the name given to the new <u>genre</u> of programs that features "real" people in "real" circumstances....

European television programmers first developed the concept of taking ordinary people and putting
5 them into unusual game-show-style situations, from which a winner would <u>emerge</u>. *Big Brother*, which confined a group of people in a small house with cameras running 24 hours a day first <u>screened</u> in Holland.

American TV networks bought some of the European
10 formats and created others themselves. Since then, reality TV has become a major phenomenon in the US [and Canada] with most major networks screening some type of reality program....

Is it a disturbing trend or light-hearted entertainment?
15 Programs such as *Survivor* and *Big Brother* [have] proved to be big winners for the networks—so what's

the attraction? For the networks, reality TV shows are a cheap alternative to other programming. No scriptwriter is required, nor paid actors or complex
20 sets, and they can rake in the ratings—compare this with the millions [of dollars] per episode required to produce a sitcom.... TV executives are constantly on the lookout for new reality formats to grab their share of the youth audience, a difficult market for advertis-
25 ers to reach.

Supporters claim they make intriguing viewing. Tired of the traditional soaps, sitcoms, and dramas, viewers enjoy watching the relationships of the contestants revealed and the chance to observe human behaviour
30 and interaction from a safe distance....

How far is too far?

How weird, treacherous, or degrading will reality programs become in a bid to maximise ratings? Those offended by reality TV claim that such programs rely
35 on invasions of privacy or placing ordinary people in increasingly extreme situations for the sake of ratings. They argue that such programs manipulate contestants, expose impressionable young audiences to distorted values, and too often rely on a formula in which
40 humiliation and voyeurism are the key ingredients.

How real is reality TV?

Critics argue "reality" programming would appear to have little in common with reality. The shows often feature a carefully selected group of people, confined
45 in an artificial environment. They are often monitored relentlessly and constrained by a range of arbitrary rules. Some ask whether television is even capable of conveying reality—does human behaviour change once under scrutiny of a camera?

50 Supporters argue that the opposite is true, saying that *Big Brother* had a representative range of young people that a wide audience identified with. It was its "reality" that made it popular.

---

(1) *genre*: style or kind of art form
(6) *emerge*: come out from
(8) *screened*: was shown on a television screen
(20) *rake in the ratings*: have many people watch the programs
(21) *episode*: a single show of an ongoing television program
(22) *sitcom*: situation comedy program
(26) *intriguing*: interesting
(29) *contestants*: people who participate in the show in hopes of winning a prize
(32) *treacherous*: dangerous
(32) *degrading*: embarrassing
(35) *invasions of privacy*: not respecting people's privacy
(37) *manipulate*: trick
(40) *humiliation*: embarrassment
(40) *voyeurism*: watching a person in a situation that should be private
(45) *monitored relentlessly*: constantly recorded on camera
(46) *arbitrary*: with no logic or reason
(49) *scrutiny*: judgment

Read the sentences below. First, identify what kind of subordinator is required in the blank: a subordinator expressing a relationship of a) time, b) manner, c) condition, d) reason, or e) contrast. Then, write an appropriate subordinator. More than one answer may be possible.

1. _____ many people believe reality TV began in the United States, it really began in Europe.

2. _____ the ratings are high, networks will continue to offer reality television programming.

3. Networks like producing reality programming _____ it is a cheap alternative to other programming.

4. Reality programs are made to look _____ _____ the contestants are in real situations.

5. Surprisingly, many people like watching reality television _____ the shows humiliate and degrade contestants.

6. _____ people stop watching reality television programs, networks will continue producing them.

7. Reality TV has become a major phenomenon in the US and Canada _____ American TV networks bought some of the European formats.

8. _____ people stop watching reality television programs, networks will stop producing them.

Exercise D

Match the beginning of the sentences in Column A with their appropriate endings in Column B.

Column A	Column B
1. Even though pop culture from other cultures is becoming more popular,	a) unless a new technology is developed to make them obsolete.
2. Though they both love movies,	b) it is fictional.
3. She wouldn't buy that fashion brand	c) the US still dominates the cultural world stage.
4. Cellphones will continue to dominate the market	d) as though the information were important.
5. The orchestra was playing	e) it begins to hype the game in the media.
6. At the end of the performance, the actors kept bowing	f) they never go to the cinema.
7. As soon as the company starts to design a new video game,	g) because it is used in many video games.
8. Japanese anime style has become popular	h) even if she had the money.
9. He memorizes trivia about his favourite superstar	i) until the audience had stopped applauding.
10. In spite of the claim that reality TV is real,	j) when the conductor collapsed.

Exercise E

Read the following text about the popularity of indie (independently released) music, then answer the questions using adverb clauses.

North America has had a notoriously poor independent music scene for years, especially when compared to that of a place such as, let's say, the UK. The biggest reason for this is the immense lack of pubs and clubs
5 that feature live music. I find this to be the case especially in my own hometown of Vancouver, BC. There is no shortage of big-name artists making their way through town to play venues such as the Commodore Ballroom, the Pacific Coliseum, and GM Place, but for
10 a band just trying to make a name for [itself], North America has been somewhat of a crapshoot. Granted, there are a few live jazz clubs here and there and on occasion a nightclub will feature a local band, but this in no way compares to the hundreds of live clubs in
15 London alone. All across North America, I have encountered the same problem: Not enough venues willing to support local, unheard-of artists.

Enter MySpace. The revolutionary network has made it possible for anyone with a microphone and an
20 Internet connection to put their music on display for millions of fans as well as other artists. MySpace truly is giving all bands a fighting chance to have their music heard by anyone who is willing to listen and the best part is, you don't need to travel all over the world
25 to hear it. Because of MySpace, I am able to listen to bands I have never heard of from the other side of the world, all from the comfort of my bedroom, living room, bathroom, wherever.

The jump in popularity of independent music is a
30 direct result of the spike in Internet usage over the last decade. Many folks believe that because the music is independent it's no good. This is not true at all, and in fact, some of the best music I have heard over the last several years has been independently released. Before
35 the use of the Internet and MySpace, the average person wouldn't give the artists the time of day but now that the music is free to preview and accessible within a matter of keystrokes, the general public, who normally couldn't be bothered with independently
40 released music, are starting to take notice.

iTunes is another program going above and beyond to feature independent music and the fact that you

need to pay to acquire their music is helping out in a big way. Many people (myself included) <u>scoffed</u> at the
45 idea of paying for music online when it's so readily available for free, but I now find myself, along with millions of others, using iTunes to buy my music. Even my technologically illiterate parents are using iTunes to revive their youth by downloading the entire Cars
50 discography. After spending days locked in my closet with my laptop and too much Ugandan coffee, it dawned on me that, if I was a young musician who wanted to make my living by sharing my personal music with the world, I would be pretty <u>chapped</u> to see
55 my hard work being swapped for free too. Is 99 cents too much to ask for a song that you really like? And if you like the band so much then shouldn't you be supporting them instead of <u>giving them the royal shaft</u>?

There is no doubt that the Internet has brought inde-
60 pendent music to the attention of the world, and it's nice to see bands with actual talent getting some recognition instead of the <u>cookie-cutter</u> <u>record label fabrications</u> that are hired to perform songs written by someone else. If things keep going the way they are going, we will no
65 doubt be hearing a lot from bands that normally would go a lifetime undiscovered. Just because the music isn't

being released by a major label doesn't mean it should be overlooked. Bradley Nowell [an American musician] once said, "Good music is good music, and that should
70 be enough for anybody," and he was right.

---

(7) *big-name artists*: popular artists
(8) *venues*: the place where a public concert happens
(11) *a crapshoot*: a gamble
(30) *spike*: large increase
(36) *give the artists the time of day*: pay attention to the artists
(44) *scoffed*: laughed in a way that shows you think something is ridiculous
(54) *chapped*: upset
(58) *giving them the royal shaft*: treating them unfairly
(62) *cookie-cutter*: predictable
(62) *record label fabrications*: bands that are not really made up of talented musicians, but that have been put together by the record companies because they have a look that appeals to the public

---

Complete the answers to the following questions using the expressions in parentheses.

1. Why has North America had a notoriously poor independent music scene?

   (local venues / support) North America has had a notoriously poor independent music scene…

   _____

   _____

2. What will Canadian venues need to do in order for the independent music scene to improve?

   (local venues / support) Canada's independent music scene will not improve…

   _____

   _____

3. With networking sites like MySpace, it is easy for independent musicians to distribute their music. When was it difficult for independent artists to distribute their music?

   (MySpace) It was difficult for independent artists to distribute their music…

   _____

   _____

4. What was the public's first reaction to the idea of paying for music online that makes the success of Apple's iTunes somewhat unexpected?

   (public's reaction / negative) Apple's iTunes is successful…

   _____

   _____

5. What effect did the availability of networking sites like MySpace have on people who wanted to record their music for the public?

   (networking sites / available) _____

   _____

   anyone with a microphone and Internet connection could record their music for the public.

6. What has happened as a result of independent music becoming more accessible?

   (independent music / accessible) _____

   _____

   people are beginning to take notice.

One Step Beyond—Create an Activity

Exercise F

Humans around the world have always been fascinated by heroes. People and animals with superhuman powers are as common in the traditional myths and religious stories of the past as they are in today's books, comics, films, and television programs. In small teams, create a new superhero character to share with your classmates.

Personal Data: give your hero a name, an identity, and a history

Description: describe your hero's appearance, character traits, and special powers. You may wish to include an illustration.

Guiding principles: list the moral principles that guide the actions of your hero

Action Narrative: create a story in which your character demonstrates heroic behaviour. You may wish to write your story or create a cartoon. In your story or cartoon, use at least five sentences with adverb clauses.

EXAMPLE: [adverb clause]
Frederick has superhuman strength <u>as long as he wears his baseball cap</u>.

<u>As soon as he removes his cap</u>, his powers disappear.
          [adverb clause]

Vocabulary 2

Exercise A

Complete each of the following sentences with an appropriate idiomatic expression from the list. Each sentence contains clues about the meaning of the idiomatic expression that is missing. Underline the clue that explains the idiomatic expression.

come to light	muddy the waters
deal with	poke fun at
get out of hand	shut out
get the hang of	take charge of
hang out with / at / in	the faint of heart

1. Many fans think that some humiliation of contestants in reality television programs is okay as long as it doesn't _____. Too much humiliation is unacceptable.

2. Reality shows like *Vanity Insanity*, which showcases surgeries that people undergo to make themselves look beautiful, is not for _____.
If you cannot watch scenes with blood and bruising, then you should not watch this show.

3. Critics of reality television sometimes _____ the contestants. While it's not nice to laugh at other people's misfortunes, sometimes contestants behave in ridiculous ways.

4. It must be difficult for Hollywood celebrities to _____ being superstars. They are constantly followed, photographed, and quoted. They have no privacy at all. That must be difficult to manage.

5. I watched my favourite indie musician play her new song on YouTube. I tried to copy what she was playing on the guitar, but I couldn't _____ those difficult guitar chords. Even though I practised playing them, I just couldn't learn them.

6. Despite the fact that I have many friends on my Facebook page, there are some people that I _____. I don't invite them onto my friends list and if they contact me, I don't respond.

7. Some people prefer to _____ friends online rather than meet with friends face-to-face.

8. Networking sites on the Internet allow indie musicians to _____ their own music distribution. Because they don't have to depend on some record label to sell their music, they can be much more creative and take more risks in their music.

9. It was first thought that there was only one kind of general intelligence. However, in the last several years it has _____ that there may be multiple intelligences. The research of American psychologist Howard Gardner has revealed that there are at least eight different kinds of intelligences, including musical intelligence.

10. It's hard to understand why the celebrity committed suicide. Fans were stalking him. Tabloids were writing lies about him. Photographers were relentless in taking pictures of him in private moments. All these things make it difficult to identify a clear, single cause for his death. To _____ even more, he was also addicted to drugs. That makes it even more confusing.

Exercise B

Conversation Practice

Interview three different classmates, asking at least four of the questions below.

hang out (with)

1. Who are your favourite people to <u>hang out with</u>?

2. Where do you like to <u>hang out</u> with friends?

3. Where do you like to <u>hang out</u> at school?

deal with

1. What do people your age have to <u>deal with</u> that makes being your age challenging?

2. What are the hardest things you have to <u>deal with</u> as a learner of English?

come to light

1. What are some of the things related to education that have <u>come to light</u> for you in the last year?

2. What are some things that have <u>come to light</u> in the world of science in recent years?

take charge of

1. What kinds of things do want to <u>take charge of</u> in your life?

2. What aspects of your life do you wish you could <u>take more charge of</u>?

3. What things do you think people generally don't <u>take enough charge of</u>?

faint of heart

1. Make a list of things that you think are not for <u>the faint of heart</u>.

2. Describe the characteristics of people who are <u>faint of heart.</u>

3. Why do you think some people are <u>faint of heart</u>?

get out of hand

1. What are some of the things you've let <u>get out of hand</u> in your personal life?

2. In your opinion, what things should parents not let <u>get out of hand</u> when raising children?

3. What can <u>get out of hand</u> in a relationship that might cause a couple to break up?

poke fun at

1. What kinds of things do you like to <u>poke fun at</u>?

2. What kinds of things do young children like to <u>poke fun at</u>?

3. From your experience, what kinds of things do comedians <u>poke fun at</u>?

4. What kinds of things do you think people should not <u>poke fun at</u>?

shut out

1. What kinds of people do you <u>shut out</u> of your life?

2. What negative behaviours do you <u>shut out</u> of your life?

3. In your opinion, what kinds of people or groups are <u>shut out</u> from mainstream society?

muddy the waters

1. What are some of things that have <u>muddied the waters</u> of your life?

2. What kinds of things <u>muddy the waters</u> in your success as a student?

3. What kinds of things <u>muddy the waters</u> in a romantic relationship?

4. What kinds of things <u>muddy the waters</u> in family life?

get the hang of

1. What are ten things you'd like to <u>get the hang of</u>?

2. What are five things you've tried to <u>get the hang of,</u> but can't?

3. What are five things you think a person needs to <u>get the hang of</u> in order to be a successful student?

4. What are five things you think a person needs to <u>get the hang of</u> in order to have a good relationship with a parent?

Writing

The Essay

An essay consists of several paragraphs written about a central idea. Like paragraphs, you can write many different types of essays such as Narrative, Descriptive, Expository, Comparison and Contrast, Classification, Process, Cause and Effect, and Argumentative. The type of essay you choose will depend on your purpose for writing the essay. There are a number of common features all essays have, no matter what kind they are. For example, every essay must have a title. Although essays can have as few as three paragraphs, and may have as many paragraphs as needed, we will look at a basic five-paragraph essay. Each paragraph in the essay has a specific function.

Paragraph 1: The first paragraph serves as an introduction to the essay. It introduces the topic to be discussed, contains the thesis statement (the controlling idea of the essay), and gives some background information. In addition, it must attract the reader's attention.

Paragraphs 2–4: These are the developmental paragraphs. Depending on the type of essay being written, these main body paragraphs describe various aspects of the topic, outline causes or effects (or possibly both), indicate points of comparison or contrast, give examples, or describe processes. Each paragraph in the body has a topic sentence which clearly supports the thesis statement.

Paragraph 5: The final paragraph is the concluding paragraph. This paragraph restates or summarizes the main premise of the essay using different words than the introductory paragraph, and leaves the reader with a clear final thought.

Thesis Statement:

The thesis statement contains the controlling idea for the essay. It is a complete sentence and expresses a complete thought. It is similar to the topic sentence because it expresses an attitude, idea, or opinion about the topic that needs to be proved. The thesis statement is broader in scope than the topic sentence and expresses the controlling idea for the entire essay. The topic sentences contained in the body will all relate to the controlling idea in the thesis statement.

Steps to writing an effective essay

Before attempting to write an essay, it is necessary to follow some basic steps.

Step 1: Choose a topic and narrow the topic.
Step 2: Identify your target audience.
Step 3: Write a thesis statement.
Step 4: Brainstorm for ideas.

Note: If you are not sure what aspect of the topic you really want to write about, you will need to brainstorm before you produce your thesis statement.

Step 5: Organize your ideas into related groups and discard any that do not relate to the thesis statement.
Step 6: Write an outline for the essay.
Step 7: Ensure that all points on the outline support the thesis.
Step 8: Write the first draft of your essay.
Step 9: Revise your essay.
Step 10: Edit and give your essay a title if it doesn't already have one.
Step 11: Rewrite your essay.
Step 12: Proofread your essay.

The Outline

The outline, if done properly, may take you as much time to write as the actual essay; however, in the long run, it saves a lot of time and frustration. If you have carefully ensured that all your topic sentences support the thesis, that all the supporting details support the topic sentences, and that there are smooth transitions between the paragraphs, you'll have an effective essay that is unified and coherent. Writing an essay without an outline is like building a house without a blueprint. You may know roughly how to build the house, but unless your foundations are extremely solid and your workmanship is superb, you will be stuck with a problem house that will need a lot of repair—that is, if it doesn't just collapse altogether!

A skeleton outline for a five-paragraph essay would be as follows:

A. **Introductory Paragraph** (1)
    i) thesis statement
    ii) background information

B. **Developmental (Body) Paragraphs** (2–4)

Paragraph 2
    i) topic sentence (a complete sentence supporting some aspect of the thesis)
    ii) supporting detail(s) (supports the topic sentence and is written in words or phrases)

Paragraph 3
    i) topic sentence (a complete sentence supporting some aspect of the thesis)
    ii) supporting detail(s) (supports the topic sentence and is written in words or phrases)

Paragraph 4
    i) topic sentence (a complete sentence supporting some aspect of the thesis)
    ii) supporting detail(s) (supports the topic sentence and is written in words or phrases)

C. **Concluding Paragraph** (5)
    i) reference to, restatement of, or summary of the thesis
    ii) concluding comments

Exercise A

Read the following essay and prepare an outline of its structure by completing the chart on page 80. This essay presents a particular point of view.

Girls and Gaming

Over the last few decades, the topic of girls and gaming has become of great interest to educational researchers. Why? Simply put, girls spend less time playing computer games than boys, and researchers want to know why. Many people may think that technology and computers are simply more interesting to boys, but this does not appear to be the case. Girls and gaming is not a pop-culture issue. At an early, age girls are just as interested in computer gaming as boys, but by the age of 13, they lag behind boys in their interest in, and time spent playing, computer games. This worries educators because there are some educational benefits to playing computer games. For one thing, playing computer games increases a child's confidence in working with computers. On average, girls enter computer science courses with less confidence and computer experience than boys. Early gaming experience can motivate a person to study computer programming later on. In addition, some research suggests that girls' lack of experience and lower confidence levels can affect their success in solving problems. In one study, the confidence level of girls affected their computer-playing abilities and problem solving through trial and error in negative ways. Another educational benefit of computer gaming is improved spatial skills development. Increased video game practice can lead to improvement in spatial skills, especially for children who begin with lower-than-average spatial skills. More importantly, though, girls' lesser interest in computer gaming can be an introduction to a life in which technology plays a less significant role than it does for boys. If girls are as interested as boys in gaming, why does their participation in computer gaming decrease as they mature? Girls are not as attracted to gaming because of the negative representation of women, the violent themes, and the competitive content and design of the games.

One reason girls lose interest in computer games is that in most games, girls do not see themselves represented in positive ways. Most video game characters are male, and when female characters are used, they are often portrayed negatively. According to the research organization Children Now, only 16 percent of game characters are female and about half of the female characters are bystanders rather than active participants in the action. Furthermore, most female game characters have unnaturally large breasts, are unusually thin, or are generally scantily dressed. In addition, female video game characters often play the role of "damsel in distress" and are either victims or prizes in video games.

Another reason girls spend less time playing computer games as they get older is that the violence in many computer games does not appeal to girls over the long term. Violence in video games decreases girls' self-worth. In one study, researchers surveyed seventh-grade girls and boys about their favourite video and computer games, and the average amount of time they spent playing games each week. The researchers determined that the more time girls spent playing violent games, the lower the girls' scores on measures of social behaviour, including scholastic achievement, social acceptance, and self-esteem. In short, playing violent computer games makes girls feel bad about themselves. This does not seem to be the case for boys.

A third reason girls lose interest in gaming as they get older is that girls are not attracted to the same content and design of video games as boys. Most popular boys' games are a contest between good and evil. Girls, however, are more interested in games designed around storylines than those designed around competition, and they are more interested in exploring the characters' personalities and lives than in winning the games. Still, designers consider competition the most important concept of computer games. Girls also prefer real-life locations for stories, while boys prefer fantasy worlds. These are important differences, but they're not the only ones. Girls also have different preferences in game design. They prefer games they can play with others, either online or at the same computer. While boys do play group games, they actually prefer playing solo. The interpersonal communication and relationships that computers facilitate is the main appeal of the Internet for women. One study even found that undergraduate women primarily use the Internet for sending email whereas undergraduate males use it primarily for searching for factual information.

The gender gap in computer gaming can be explained by the fact that computer games are designed by male designers for male audiences. The implicit message that designers are sending in the way they design the content and play of games is that "there is no place for girls" in the world of computer gaming. The problem of girls and gaming is not simply a matter of girls and boys engaging in different leisure activities. Computer gaming is more than a pop-culture phenomenon. It is about encouraging girls to become equal participants in scientific and technological evolutions. The challenge is to design electronic games which appeal not only to boys, but also to girls, and which build confidence while simultaneously engaging players in sound mathematics and science activity.

THE ESSAY

Title

INTRODUCTION

Thesis Statement:

BODY

Developmental Paragraph 1

Topic Sentence:

Support:

Developmental Paragraph 2

Topic Sentence:

Support:

Developmental Paragraph 3

Topic Sentence:

Support:

CONCLUSION

Topic Sentence:

Concluding Idea:

Exercise B

If you were assigned an essay on the general topic of Popular Culture, your first step would be to narrow the topic. Fill in the circles to narrow down possible essay topics.

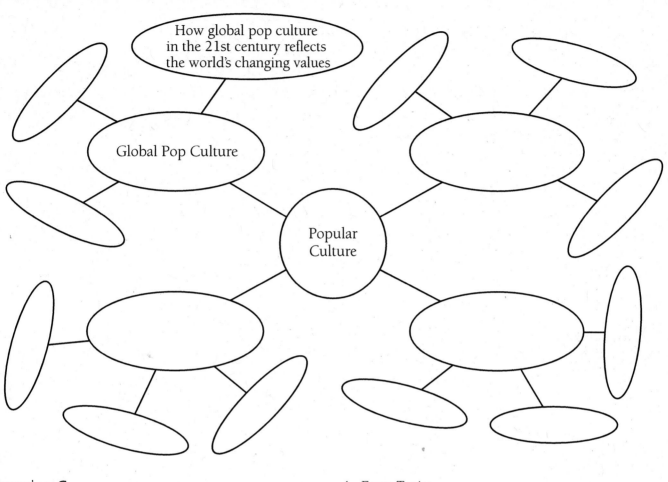

Exercise C

Thesis Statements

Choose five of your narrowed essay topics from Exercise B and write a thesis statement for each one.

1. Essay Topic:

Thesis Statement: _____

_____

_____

2. Essay Topic:

Thesis Statement: _____

_____

_____

3. Essay Topic:

Thesis Statement: _____

_____

_____

4. Essay Topic:

Thesis Statement: _____

_____

_____

5. Essay Topic:

Thesis Statement: _____

_____

_____

Exercise D

Planning the Essay

Write a point-form outline for an essay based on one of your topics from Exercise C.

Exercise E

Based on your outline in Exercise D, write an essay.

Essay Outline Checklist

- ☐ Did I brainstorm ideas?
- ☐ Have I identified my audience?
- ☐ Does my essay have a title?
- ☐ Is my topic sufficiently narrowed?
- ☐ Have I eliminated ideas that don't relate?
- ☐ Does my thesis statement contain a controlling idea (attitude)?
- ☐ Do the topic sentences in the body support my thesis?
- ☐ Do I have at least two to three points to illustrate the main point made in each of my topic sentences?

Academic Word List

access	distribution	network
alternative	emphasis	occur
comments	export	physical
communication	features	primary
considerable	illustrated	sought
constitutional	individual	specified
convention	investment	

Exercise A

Word Meaning

Match each underlined word or phrase from the sentences in Column A with the appropriate word in Column B.

Part A

Column A	Column B
1. The director <u>looked for</u> a new actor to play James Bond.	a) access
2. I can't remember the name of the <u>person</u> who told me about the movie.	b) alternative
3. Indie music is an<u>(other) option</u> to commercially produced music.	c) communication
4. I'm surprised at how popular this actress is, because her <u>bodily</u> appearance is unpleasant.	d) constitution
5. My <u>connection based on a common interest</u> of friends on the Internet is worldwide.	e) emphasize
6. The James Bond movies <u>draw more attention to</u> action rather than the relationships between characters.	f) features
7. What <u>descriptions</u> do you think define the manga style of animation?	g) individual
8. Girls use the Internet more for <u>the process of sharing information</u> than for searching for factual information.	h) network
9. The Internet allows people to <u>get</u> much more information than any library does.	i) physical
10. Canada has a <u>group of laws that gives the country's people specific rights and responsibilities.</u>	j) sought

Part B

Column A	Column B
11. Lumber is Canada's most important <u>product sold and delivered outside its borders.</u>	k) comments
12. Greeting <u>patterns of behaviour</u> differ across cultures.	l) considerable
13. The <u>common and important</u> role female characters play in computer games is the role of "damsel in distress."	m) conventions n) distribution
14. What do you think would <u>happen</u> if television screenwriters went on strike for a whole year?	o) export p) illustrated
15. The band did not <u>say specifically</u> how much it earned from that concert.	q) investment r) occur
16. Did you read the negative <u>statements</u> the reporter made about that celebrity?	s) primary t) specify
17. The manga artist <u>drew and showed</u> the character's emotions in her large eyes.	
18. Without networking sites on the Internet, the <u>spread</u> of indie music would be very limited.	
19. The <u>money spent in order to make a profit</u> in the film was substantial.	
20. Famous musicians earn a <u>great</u> amount of money.	

Exercise B
Pronunciation—Syllables and Stress

Listen to your teacher or an audio dictionary to hear the pronunciation for each word in the list. Repeat each word aloud. Mark the syllables and major word stress.

1.   access (v): **ăc** / cess
2.   alternative (n): _____
3.   comments (n): _____
4.   communication (n): _____
5.   considerable (adj): _____
6.   constitutional (adj): _____
7.   convention (n): _____
8.   distribution (n): _____
9.   emphasis (n): _____
10   export (n): _____
11.   features (n): _____
12.   illustrated (v): _____
13.   individual (n): _____
14.   investment (n): _____
15.   network (n): _____
16.   occur (v): _____
17.   physical (adj): _____

18.   primary (adj): _____
19.   sought (v): _____
20.   specified (v): _____

Exercise C
Word Forms

Fill in each blank with the word form indicated in parentheses. More than one word may be possible for each indicated word form.

1.   access (v): _____ (n)
     _____ (adj)
2.   alternative (n): _____ (v)
     _____ (adj)
3.   comments (n): _____ (v)
4.   communication (n): _____ (v)
     _____ (adj)
5.   considerable (adj): _____ (n)
     _____ (v) _____ (adv)
6.   constitutional (adj): _____ (n)
7.   convention (n): _____ (v)
     _____ (adj)
8.   distribution (n): _____ (v)
9.   emphasis (n): _____ (v)

10. export (n): _____ (v)
    _____ (adj)

11. features (n): _____ (v)
    _____ (adj)

12. illustrated (v): _____ (n)
    _____ (adj)

13. individual (n): _____ (v)
    _____ (adj) _____ (adv)

14. investment (n): _____ (v)
    _____ (adj)

15. network (n): _____ (v)
    _____ (adj)

16. occur (v): _____ (n)

17. physical (adj): _____ (adv)

18. primary (adj): _____ (adv)

19. specified (v): _____ (n)
    _____ (adj) _____ (adv)

Exercise D

In a dictionary, find one example sentence for each word in Exercise A and copy it into your notebook. Draft a second sentence of your own. Then, work with a partner to revise and edit your sentence.

Exercise E

Read the following story and complete each blank with one of the words from the list. You do not have to change the grammatical form of any of the words. Use each word only once.

alternative	features	investment
exports		

We live in a truly global culture and although the US still dominates the world pop-culture stage, things are changing. India 1 _____ its Bollywood films around the world; the distinctive 2 _____ of the manga anime style are found globally in comics, film, and video games; and world music offers an intriguing 3 _____ to the commercial British and US music scene. Despite the vast 4 _____ of North American production companies in pop-culture products, the world market is beginning to demand more.

access	conventions	networks
communication	distribution	primarily

The explosion of international pop culture is 5 _____ made possible through the enhanced 6 _____ channels of the Internet. Online 7 _____ allow fans to 8 _____ cultural products they never could before. Indie musicians are posting their music on social networking pages. Independent film producers are putting their work online as well. Large production companies are no longer controlling the 9 _____ of pop-culture products. The 10 _____ of producing culture products are slowly changing as a result of increased participation in the production of music, film and writing at the grassroots level.

commentary	illustrated	sought
considerable	individual	specified
constitutional	occurs	

This new trend in cultural production is best 11 _____ by the exploding popularity of blogging. Not only can any 12 _____ blog his or her own view of events and states in the world, but the work of reputable writers and journalists is 13 _____ out by millions of readers who want a 14 _____ that is not spun by the magazines and publishers that have traditionally controlled the flow of ideas. In a way, blogging is a form of resistance to the 15 _____ power and control that mainstream media have had on public opinion. Many Americans and Canadians consider blogging a 16 _____ right because of the free speech implications. Free speech is a 17 _____ right in both the US and Canadian constitutions. Freedom of expression has its greatest benefits when it 18 _____ in an environment of diversity of opinions and ideas. So once again, we see that pop culture is more than simply trends, fads, and fancies. Pop culture reflects the values of human societies, and the global distribution of international pop culture is surely a good thing.

Unit 8
It's How You Play the Game

Vocabulary

Exercise A

Match the idioms in Column A with their definitions in Column B.

Column A	Column B
1. ballpark figure	a) getting worse and worse
2. beat me to the punch	b) acting tough
3. bounce a few ideas off you	c) deal with a difficult situation
4. clear sailing	d) do something before I get a chance to do it
5. going downhill	e) no problems in sight
6. go the distance	f) equal in a race
7. neck and neck	g) to try something difficult
8. playing hardball	h) tell you something in order to get your opinion
9. to tackle	i) approximate value
10. wrestle with the hard facts	j) able to finish what you start

Exercise B

Complete the following dialogue using the idioms from Exercise A.

Ray: Annie, I'd like to ₁ _____ you.

Annie: What's on your mind Ray? Are you thinking about the possibility that we might lose the farm?

Ray: Actually, I was thinking about baseball. I want to build a diamond in our backyard. It would be a big job ₂ _____, but something is telling me it's the right thing to do.

Annie: Are you crazy? The bank is about to foreclose on our mortgage. They are really ₃ _____. They've already told you if you don't come up with the back payments within two months, they'll take the farm from us.

Ray: Look, I know that since we moved here it has not all been ₄ _____ for us. I have a gut feeling that things are going to work out for us even though it looks like it's all ₅ _____ at this point. Your support would really mean a lot to me.

Annie: Give me a ₆ _____—how much would this dream of yours set us back?

Ray: About five grand by the time I add the bleachers and the lights.

Annie: Ray, I think it's time you ₇ _____. We can't even afford this farm, let alone sinking $5000 we don't have into a baseball field in the middle of nowhere.

Ray: Annie—trust me. There's a voice in my head telling me that if I build it they will come.

Annie: Who will come? I think you've finally gone off the deep end.

Ray: Trust me Annie. ₈ _____ with me and you will see—they will come.

Vocabulary Expansion 1

Exercise C

Gita is a camp counsellor this summer. She has been put in charge of the sports program because she said that she knew a lot about sports. Her first task is to pick up the equipment the camp will need for the various activities. The wholesaler where she is purchasing the items has everything in the back warehouse so Gita must ask specifically for everything she wants. Gita's problem is that although she knows what the equipment looks like or what it is used for, she can never remember the actual names of the items. Identify the items that Gita is trying to purchase. Identify the three sports that Gita will play at the camp this summer.

1. I guess I'll need 8 of those webbed things. You know— the ones with the flat round head on a long thin handle. We're not professionals so nylon strings will be okay.

2. Do you carry those leather hand covers used to catch those round things? I'll need 18 right-handed ones and 2 left-handed ones.

3. I'd better take 2 of those round leather things you blow up with the pump. All that kicking gives them quite a beating. I guess the official European size would be the best.

4. Please give me a half dozen of those smooth long wooden sticks. Maybe I'd better take a dozen in case a few of them get cracked if someone hits hard. Better yet, do you have any aluminum ones?

5. Do you carry those special covers for feet that have those points on the bottom for better traction so you don't fall when you go to kick if the grass is wet? Actually, I'll have to wait to get those because I don't know what sizes to buy.

6. I'll need at least a dozen of those cone-shaped things with the rubber tips. How much more are the ones that have real feathers than the ones made of plastic?

Sports: 1. _____

2. _____

3. _____

One Step Beyond—Create an Activity
Exercise D

You have the same job as Gita, but like Gita, you don't know the names of the equipment. Choose at least two sports you will play at your camp, and write descriptions for at least ten pieces of equipment. Bring the descriptions to class and exchange them with a classmate. Try to name the equipment described and determine the sport being played.

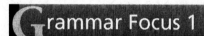

Grammar Focus 1

GERUNDS (base + *ing*)
Exercise A

Complete the following with a gerund or gerund phrase.

1. I really regret not _____
2. He has always avoided _____
3. We discussed _____
4. As a teenager, I disliked not _____
5. Did they mention _____
6. Soccer players have to practise _____
7. I can't imagine not _____
8. Star athletes can't risk _____

Exercise B

Use verbs that are followed by gerunds such as *imagine, keep, can't help, understand, suggest,* and *don't agree,* in order to express your opinion about the following statements.

EXAMPLE: With all the improvements in equipment,

hockey is a very safe sport to play.

I can't help wondering why so many players still lose their front teeth.

1. All sports are elitist because only people with money can afford to play them.

_____

_____

2. Professional wrestling is a true sport, and not a lot of overacting as many people believe.

_____

_____

3. Girls and boys should not take part in mixed teams.

_____

_____

4. Individual sports are more challenging than team sports.

_____

_____

5. Many people do not consider synchronized swimming to be a sport that should be in the Olympics.

_____

_____

Exercise C

Change the infinitives of purpose in the following sentences to a *by* + gerund phrase.

EXAMPLE: Professional tennis players practise their serves daily to improve their accuracy.

Professional tennis players improve their accuracy *by practising their serves daily.*

1. The figure skater sharpened his skates to increase his speed.

_____

_____

2. Tony ran the fastest race of his life to win the Olympic 100-metre dash.

_____

_____

3. Ken changed the wax on his skis to accommodate the changing snow conditions.

_____

_____

4. Michael restrung his racquet to ensure it was in top shape.

_____

_____

5. The baseball player caught a fly ball to end the game.

_____

_____

6. Chandra bowled a perfect game to win the tournament.

_____

_____

Exercise D

Join the following pairs of sentences by beginning each new sentence with the words in italics.

EXAMPLE: Physical sports like tennis build cardio endurance.
Tennis is appropriate for this.

Tennis is appropriate for building cardio endurance.

1. Ken isn't sure he'll be able to afford his son's hockey equipment. *Ken is concerned about* this.

_____

_____

2. I'm going to Wimbledon to watch the tennis finals. *I'm very excited about* this.

_____

_____

3. Eric scores a lot of goals. *He is very good at* it.

_____

_____

4. They have the most Olympic medals for rowing won by any Canadian. *Marnie McBean and Kathleen Heddle are really proud of* that.

_____

_____

5. The hockey team enjoys playing on the new ice surface. *The new arena is very suitable for* that.

_____

_____

6. Juan and Kalil always argue when they play tennis. *They are tired of* this.

_____

_____

7. They must win the next game to make the playoffs. *The team is worried about* it.

_____

_____

8. Liam can't dive from the high board. *He's afraid of* doing it.

_____

_____

Exercise E

Fill in the blanks with a preposition + gerund.

1. This summer I am planning _____ _____ swimming at least three times a week.

2. Instead _____ _____ at home to watch TV, I plan to be more active.

3. I'm looking forward _____ _____ a little weight and getting into better shape.

4. I'm not good _____ _____ to exercise plans. I usually give up after a week.

5. In spite _____ _____ in the past, I'm going to give it my best shot.

Exercise F

Join the following pairs of sentences by beginning each new sentence with the words in italics.

EXAMPLE: They were playing tennis. That's how *we left them*.

We left them playing tennis.

1. The park attendant likes draining the wading pool half an hour early. *We can't have him* doing that.

_____

_____

2. The referee is constantly making calls in favour of the other team. *I resent* that.

_____

_____

3. Jolene is playing at the top of her game during this tournament. *Everyone appreciates* that.

_____

_____

4. The neighbourhood children like playing road hockey on our street. *I don't mind them* doing that.

_____

_____

5. Shari is giving them swimming lessons. *They appreciate her* doing that.

_____

_____

Exercise G

Complete the following passage with the appropriate gerund forms of five of the following verbs: *return, plan, reward, swim, dive, dart, excite, hope*. Identify the types of gerunds.

I went scuba diving on the Great Barrier Reef. I was 1 _____ to see lots of colourful tropical fish. Luckily, I was able to enjoy 2 _____ alongside plenty of beautiful fish. 3 _____ on the Reef was definitely one of the highlights of my vacation in Australia. Being able to photograph the fish was 4 _____ . I plan on 5 _____ there on my next vacation.

Grammar in Use

Exercise H

Look at the following points about the advantages and disadvantages of choosing either golf or tennis as your sporting activity of choice.

Tennis

- requires only a racquet and tennis balls to play
- must be played with a partner or group of four
- requires a certain amount of physical fitness and endurance
- is a fast-paced sport requiring total concentration
- allows little socializing time while playing
- competitive games are only possible when playing against someone of equal ability
- requires many areas of athletic ability, including speed, hand-eye coordination, strategy, strength, and endurance
- provides physical and cardiovascular benefits

Golf

- requires golf clubs, balls, and tees (Golf clubs can be rented.)
- can be played without a partner or group
- accommodates any physical characteristics of the athlete
- allows people to slow down and think about other things
- allows players to socialize while playing
- allows poor players to play competitively against good players because of the handicap system
- provides a leisurely walk and no real physical strain

Using the information above, complete the following sentences with gerund phrases.

EXAMPLE: People who have busy, stressful jobs enjoy

_____

People who have busy, stressful jobs enjoy playing golf because it allows them to relax.

1. If a tennis player enjoys a competitive game, she should avoid

2. People who are not in good physical shape should avoid

3. Golf is for people who enjoy

4. Tennis is for people who enjoy

5. Golf is for people who dislike

6. Tennis is for people who dislike

7. Tennis players are interested in

8. Golf players are interested in

9. Tennis players can take advantage of

10. Golf players can take advantage of

One Step Beyond—Create an Activity

Exercise I

Create a questionnaire to administer to at least five different people from different age groups. Survey their likes and dislikes about sports on TV and sports they like to participate in. Compile the statistics from your survey and write at least ten sentences about the results, using gerunds or gerund phrases. Leave a blank for the gerund and exchange your exercise with a classmate.

EXAMPLE   Teenagers detest _____ golf on TV with their parents. Answer: having to watch

Vocabulary Expansion 2

Exercise A

Match the sports verbs in Column A with the definitions in Column B.

Column A		Column B	
1.	ride	a)	to lie on the surface of water
2.	dribble	b)	to put the bike on one tire and rotate
3.	jump	c)	to throw the ball into the basket with force
4.	slam	d)	to transfer the ball to a teammate
5.	serve	e)	to move along the snow smoothly
6.	splash	f)	to move the ball forward by bouncing it
7.	smash	g)	to kick
8.	glide	h)	to lift off a ramp into the air
9.	boot	i)	to sit on a bike and move it by pedaling
10.	float	j)	to hit very hard
11.	spin	k)	to scatter water with your hands or feet
12.	pass	l)	to hit the ball over the net into play

Exercise B

Complete the following spidermaps with verbs associated with the sports identified in the circles. For each sport, include at least two verbs from the list in Exercise A. Look in the sports section of the newspaper, a sports magazine, sports web pages on the Internet, or listen to a sports commentary on TV or on the radio for possible words.

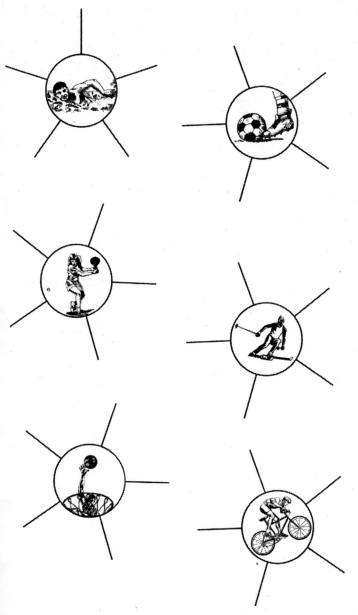

Exercise C

Write a sentence about each sport using at least one of the verbs associated with the sport that you identified in Exercise B.

Exercise D

Although many sports have different words associated with them that describe certain actions or objects, if a precise word does not exist, adjectives can be used to show the degree of intensity. Insert the following intensifiers in the chart below.

a bit	kind of	reasonably
a little	much	slightly
a touch	pretty	somewhat
awfully	quite	sort of
considerably	rather	substantially
extremely	really	very

Degree of Intensity	Intensifiers
A small degree	
A moderate degree	
A large degree	

Exercise E

Complete the following sentences by adding an appropriate intensifier.

1. Jamil is _____ out of shape. He hasn't been able to exercise since his accident a month ago.

2. Carter hit the ball _____ hard. It went right out of the park.

3. The crowd was _____ subdued. The home team was in a real slump.

4. The putt was _____ short of the hole. Another few centimetres and he would have birdied.

5. Ken has _____ improved his game since taking lessons from a pro.

6. Helga is _____ talented but not enough to turn professional.

Grammar Focus 2

INFINITIVES (*to* + base)

Exercise A

Read the following text about some popular extreme sports, and then answer the questions using infinitive forms.

Ultimate Frisbee

Ultimate Frisbee is a non-contact sport played by two teams of seven. The sport can be played on any surface, but it is usually played on grass. The field is approximately 110 metres long. One teammate throws a disc to another teammate, trying to move the disc down the length of the field. Players trying to catch the disc try to run into an open position on the field where they can catch the disc without interference from the other team. Members of the team try to pass the disc to a teammate in the opponent's end zone. The opposing team tries to get the disc. If a player is in the opposing team's end zone and catches the disc, the team scores a goal. The player cannot run into the end zone while holding the disc—he or she must catch it while already in the end zone.

The rules are:

- The team consists of three males, three females, and a seventh player of either gender.
- If the disc is dropped or goes out of bounds, the other team is given possession of the disc.
- Players are not allowed to take any steps once they have possession of the disc—they have to move the disc by passing. If they take a step, the disc is turned over to the other team.
- Each team is allowed time outs.
- A player can be substituted after a goal is scored or when a player is injured.
- The disc may be thrown in any direction.
- A goal is worth one point. At the end of the game, the team with the most points is the winner.

Street Luge

Street luge is an individual competitive sport. Using the power of gravity, riders dressed in protective clothing and helmets lie flat on a street-luge board (which looks like a big skateboard) and rade down a paved course feet first. By lying flat, the racers decrease wind resistance and increase their speeds. The racecourse is often located on mountain roads, but occasionally races are held on city streets. Over the course, which is between one and five kilometres in length, lugers reach speeds of up to 115 kilometres per hour. Lugers use shifts in body weight to control the movement of their boards. They use their shoes to brake and control the sled. The luger with fastest time wins the race.

The rules are:

- Luge boards cannot have any mechanical brakes.
- Riders must wear leather or Kevlar racing suits and gloves, a hard helmet with a chin strap, a face shield or goggles, and sturdy shoes.

Questions

1. What is the object of ultimate Frisbee?
2. According to the rules for ultimate Frisbee, why do players try to catch the disc in the opposing team's end zone?
3. What should players do when a teammate is trying to throw the disc?
4. Why do lugers lie flat on the luge board?
5. In street luge, why are racers required to wear helmets and leather race suits?
6. For what purpose do lugers wear sturdy shoes?

Exercise B

Complete the following sentences using an infinitive.

EXAMPLE: Sarin knows she needs strong serves and returns to be a competitive volleyball player. She thinks it's essential _to practise her backhand_.

1. Rowing in the Olympics has always been my dream. I hope

2. All elite athletes follow a strict training schedule. I plan

3. Martin is really into watching the Olympic games. He finds it interesting

4. Although the star centre basketball player is slightly injured, the coach plans

5. Barbara has always dreamed of standing on the Olympic podium. She is determined

6. Xian's school is having a former Olympic athlete come to speak to them about his Olympic experience. Xian is excited

Exercise C

Use the list of verbs on the next page, in their infinitive form, to complete the following passage. Then complete the five statements that follow, using information from the passage.

consider	participate	stand
follow	perform	take part
hire	qualify	train

₁ _____ in the Olympics must be an incredible thrill. As we watch the events on television, we often forget ₂ _____ the months, if not years, of practice that have taken place in order for the athletes ₃ _____ on the podium representing their country. They have sacrificed their social lives and family time ₄ _____ a gruelling training schedule. It costs a lot of money ₅ _____ the best coaches in order to advance the athlete's career. Participation in tournaments is required ₆ _____ for a position on the Olympic team. These tournaments have given the athletes opportunities ₇ _____ their sport in front of large crowds, but nothing can compare to the Olympics themselves. In the end, only three individuals or groups will stand on those podiums, but one must keep in mind that everyone who gets ₈ _____ in the Olympics is a winner.

a) Olympic athletes are expected _____

b) It is very expensive _____

c) _____ is a thrill of a lifetime.

d) It is important _____

e) The athletes need _____

Grammar in Use
Exercise D

Underline at least eight infinitives or gerunds in the following passage.

Athletes keep getting better every year with the improvement of training facilities and equipment. Existing world records are broken on a regular basis. Many athletes, desperate to win the glory of the gold, turn to performance-enhancing drugs, such as steroids and other forms of what the athletes hope will be untraceable drugs. Regular drug testing of athletes is now a requirement in the highly competitive world of athletics. The number of records that have been awarded to athletes who have managed to slip by the testing is unclear. However, what remains a little-changed fact is the average age of top-performing athletes. In the early 1900s, the average age of gold medal winners was 25. Today, this average has changed only slightly to 24.6.

This indicates that no matter what athletes do to improve their training, equipment, or performance, age will probably be the most influential factor.

Based on the information in the paragraph, complete the following sentences with a logical gerund or infinitive phrase.

1. Athletes are determined _____

2. _____ an illegal way to enhance performance.

3. Many athletes are desperate _____

4. Officials are forced _____

5. Athletes are willing to risk _____

One Step Beyond—Create an Activity
Exercise E

Find a short, interesting article in the sports section of a newspaper or magazine. Rewrite the article leaving a blank for every infinitive. At the bottom of the article, write at least five questions which require an infinitive in the answer. Exchange your exercise with a classmate.

Writing

Introductory Paragraphs

The introduction of an essay is generally one paragraph long. The paragraph introduces the topic to be developed in the rest of the essay. It contains the thesis statement and background information, and indicates how the topic will be developed. Therefore, the introductory paragraph will indicate the kind of essay you are writing (such as descriptive, narrative, cause and effect, process, or comparison and contrast). It is important that the introductory paragraph contain information that the reader will find interesting or intriguing so the reader will want to continue to read the rest of the essay. It is not advisable to open the essay with the thesis because providing an opinion immediately does not necessarily entice the reader to read on. There are four main approaches that writers use when writing an introductory paragraph.

1. **Attention Grabber:** Start the essay with a very interesting example pertinent to the topic.

2. **Quotation:** Start the essay with an interesting quotation that relates to the topic.

3. **Opposite:** Start the essay with a statement that is actually contrary to the thesis.

4. **Cone:** Start the essay with general details and then progress to specific points.

Exercise A

Look at the following introductory paragraphs. Identify the paragraph that contains all the items in the Introductory Paragraph Checklist that follows Exercise C.

1. Many new sports are being added to the Olympics regularly. Despite recent controversy, sports such as bowling and synchronized swimming have been added to the games. This isn't a good idea in my opinion.

2. You really have to be a non-socializing introvert to want to dedicate yourself totally to becoming the best at a sport. Long hours of practice take up the time you would normally be spending with friends. Casual dates and get-togethers are impossible, especially before gruelling schedules. Athletes have the chance to meet many people from all over the world at tournaments. They become champions in their local communities, often visiting local schools to promote sports and hard work. Athletes are dedicated individuals who usually positively influence people around them with their community service and dedication to the sport.

3. In an event unprecedented in professional wrestling, Mike Tyson bit Evander Holyfield's car, bringing the match—and his career—to a stunning end. What new low has professional athletics been dragged down to when boxers, earning millions of dollars for ten rounds in a ring whether they win or not, temporarily lose it and turn into animals? Was it the pressure of the media hype surrounding the match? Was it a case of temporary insanity in which he totally lost control? Was it consciously done in the hopes that somehow he might win? No matter what the cause, Tyson's disgraceful behaviour cannot be tolerated or forgiven.

4. "I didn't take any drugs," the athlete said, as the medal was stripped from him. The adamant denial of wrongdoing gave fans a glimmer of hope. As the day passed, and the tests were verified, the disgraceful truth was confirmed. Another athlete had used steroids to enhance his performance. The honeymoon that he briefly enjoyed with his fans was over, as a nation hung its head in shame.

Exercise B

Look at paragraph 3 in Exercise A and identify the following.

1. Thesis statement
2. Approach
3. Background Info
4. Kind of Essay (rhetorical mode)
5. Point of view (controlling idea)

Exercise C

1. Write a thesis statement for each of the following topics.
2. Write introductory paragraphs using the thesis statements. Use a different approach for each paragraph.

   a) The Major Changes in the Olympics in the Last 100 Years
   b) World Competitions
   c) Taking Sports to the Extreme
   d) The Glory of the Gold

Use the Introductory Paragraph Checklist to ensure your paragraph is complete.

☑ Introductory Paragraph Checklist

☐ Will my paragraph get the reader's attention?

☐ Does my paragraph contain a thesis statement which indicates my point of view?

☐ Does my paragraph use one of the four main approaches: attention grabber, quotation, opposite, or cone?

☐ Does my introductory paragraph provide some background information?

☐ Does my introductory paragraph indicate the kind of essay that I will develop?

Academic Word List

academic	demonstrate	required
achieve	established	select
analysis	financial	subsequent
annual	focus	symbolic
aspects	injury	technical
commitment	professional	traditional
subsequent	regulations	

Exercise A

Word meaning

Match each word in Column A with the appropriate definition in Column B.

Part A

Column A	Column B
1. technical	a) willingness to give time and energy to something
2. required	b) to show something
3. academic	c) related to money matters
4. traditional	d) relating to practical skills needed for an activity
5. achieve	e) rules or laws
6. focus	f) usual way of behaving
7. demonstrate	g) related to studying and thinking
8. commitment	h) needed, essential
9. financial	i) to obtain or accomplish
10. regulations	j) to concentrate

Part B

Column A	Column B
11. analysis	k) to choose
12. symbolic	l) related to a job that requires a high level of training
13. professional	m) caused to be accepted
14. aspects	n) parts of a situation
15. subsequent	o) to succeed in reaching something
16. injury	p) examination of something in detail
17. select	q) happening yearly
18. established	r) happening after something
19. annual	s) representing something
20. achieve	t) harm to body caused by accident

Exercise B

Pronunciation—Syllable & Stress

Listen to your teacher or an audio dictionary to hear the pronunciation for each word in the list. Repeat each word aloud. Mark the syllables and major word stress.

1. academic (adj): ac / a / **dem** / ic
2. achieve (v): _____
3. analysis (n): _____
4. annual (adj): _____
5. aspects (n): _____
6. commitment (n): _____
7. concentration (n): _____
8. demonstrate (v): _____
9. established (adj): _____
10. financial (adj): _____
11. focus (v): _____
12. injury (n): _____
13. professional (adj): _____
14. regulations (n): _____
15. required (adj): _____
16. select (v): _____
17. subsequent (adj): _____
18. symbolic (adj): _____
19. technical (adj): _____
20. traditional (adj): _____

Exercise C
Word Forms

Fill in each blank with the word form indicated in parentheses. More than one word may be possible for each indicated word form.

1. academic (adj): _____ (n)
   _____ (adv)

2. achieve (v): _____ (n)
   _____ (adj)

3. analysis (n): _____ (v)
   _____ (adj) _____ (adv)

4. annual (adj): _____ (adv)

5. commitment (n): _____ (v)
   _____ (adj)

6. concentration (n): _____ (v)
   _____ (adj)

7. demonstrate (v): _____ (n)
   _____ (adj) _____ (adv)

8. established (adj): _____ (n)
   _____ (v)

9. financial (adj): _____ (n)
   _____ (v) _____ (adv)

10. focus (v): _____ (n)

11. injury (n): _____ (v)
    _____ (adj)

12. professional (adj): _____ (n)
    _____ (adv)

13. regulations (n): _____ (v)
    _____ (adj)

14. required (adj): _____ (n)
    _____ (v)

15. select (v): _____ (n)
    _____ (adj) _____ (adv)

16. symbolic (adj): _____ (n)
    _____ (v) _____ (adv)

17. technical (adj): _____ (n)
    _____ (adv)

18. traditional (adj): _____ (n)
    _____ (adv)

Exercise D

In a dictionary, find one example sentence for each word in Exercise A, Column A, and copy it into your notebook. Draft a second sentence of your own. Then, work with a partner to revise and edit your sentence.

Exercise E

Read the following story and complete each blank with one of the words from the list. You do not have to change the grammatical form of any of the words. Use each word only once.

achievable	demonstrated	professional
aspects	established	symbol
commitment	focused	technical
concentrate	injury	

Elite athletes have 1 _____ a 2 _____ to being the best they can be at their sports. They have set 3 _____ goals for themselves and 4 _____ set routines to help them reach the top of their sport. 5 _____ athletes are extremely 6 _____ on constantly improving their 7 _____ skills. They understand that they must be in top physical shape and they need to be careful to avoid 8 _____ that could potentially end their career. While they are training, they 9 _____ almost exclusively on their sport and often put other 10 _____ of their lives on hold. Elite athletes are a real 11 _____ of what can be achieved when one focuses on reaching the top.

academies	non-traditional	selected
analysis	regulated	subsequently
annual	regulations	traditional
financial		

Most sports are 12 _____ by governing bodies. These organizations are responsible for establishing the 13 _____ that govern the sport, running tournaments, and record-keeping. 14 _____, these organizations also trigger 15 _____ implications for the athletes. Usually there are 16 _____ membership fees that individual athletes or teams are required to pay in order to participate in the sport. Some sports organizations also offer sports 17 _____ for athletes who have been 18 _____ because of their potential. After an 19 _____ of the athletes' techniques, the instructors plan individual programs so the athletes can hone their skills. The trainers combine both 20 _____ and 21 _____ methods to support the athletes' development.

Unit 9
Food for Thought

Vocabulary

atmosphere	impulse	perishable
diversification	interloper	tread
enticement	onslaught	unique
govern		

Exercise A

Complete each of the following sentences with a form of one of the vocabulary words listed above.

1. Her _____ behaviour amused her friends but worried her parents.

2. Despite valiant efforts on behalf of the firefighters, two people _____ in the fire.

3. The _____ pressure is making my head ache.

4. Her _____ outlook on life makes her a very interesting person to be with.

5. The _____ against government cutbacks has never been witnessed in this country before.

6. The _____ came in, interrupted the meeting, gave his unwanted opinion, and left.

7. Helga has such a heavy _____ that she could wake the dead if she walked across their graves.

8. The _____ has been creating some very unpopular policies lately.

9. Our investment manager suggested that we _____ our portfolio to ensure we don't risk everything on one stock.

10. All the candies placed at the supermarket checkout are there to _____ children to want junk food.

Exercise B

The $2500 Pyramid

Each block of the pyramid below contains a list of words or phrases which relate to a form of the vocabulary words from Listening 1 (Before You Listen #3) on page 143 in the Student Book. Award yourself the monetary value for each word you guess correctly. Then, write a sentence for each of your answers. The sentence should demonstrate your understanding of the word.

EXAMPLE:

```
$200
get rid of
remove
eliminate
```

Answer: Things that relate to "eradicate"

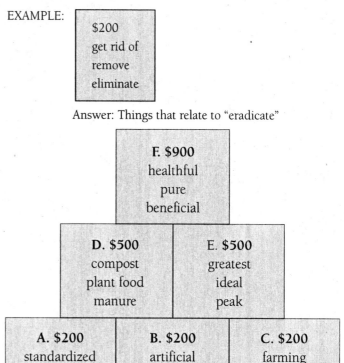

F. $900
healthful
pure
beneficial

D. $500
compost
plant food
manure

E. $500
greatest
ideal
peak

A. $200
standardized
controlled
ruled

B. $200
artificial
man-made
unnatural

C. $200
farming
gardening
planting

Exercise C
Expansion Activity

Fill in the blanks in the reading with the following words.

antioxidants	genetically	rotate
compost	healthier	standards
condition	organic	sustaining
depletion	organizations	synthetic
fertilizers	residual	urban

Organic Food—What is it Really?

Have you walked into a grocery store and looked at the produce aisle lately? Chances are good that if you live in an 1 _____ setting, your local grocery store offers the choice of both traditionally grown and organi- cally grown fruits and vegetables. You might notice that even though the 2 _____ produce may not look as nice as the other produce for sale in the store, it prob- ably costs significantly more.

Consumers are often advised to purchase organic produce if they want to improve their health. You might hear claims that organic produce not only tastes better, but has more 3 _____, which are sup- posed to kill cancer-causing free radicals in your sys- tem. Also, because the fruits and vegetables are grown organically, they are supposed to have more vitamins and minerals, and no 4 _____ pesticides. But can you really believe these claims?

Are all organics created equal? If the product's label says it is organic, is the food really 5 _____ for us? There are many products that food producers claim are organic, but until recently there have been no strict guidelines as to what can actually be labelled as certi- fied organic. There are now several 6 _____ that certify organic farmers who adhere to predeter- mined organic 7 _____. These farmers have to pass an independent inspection of their farms and keep careful records of their farming process to be able to use the "certified organic" label.

Organic farmers are generally committed to 8 _____ the viability of the land. This is done through careful crop rotation and by allowing periods of rest for the soil, to prevent 9 _____ of essen- tial minerals in the soil. When selecting their seeds for planting, these farmers use seeds that have been natu- rally gathered from crops, rather than seeds that have been 10 _____ engineered to produce superior products. There is a lot of controversy surrounding the use of genetically modified seeds because many people believe that by tampering with nature, we are possibly altering the genetic codes of plants, and that this could possibly trigger cancer and other diseases. Additionally, instead of using 11 _____ chemicals—which some claim are harmful to our health—to supplement the soil, organic farmers use natural fertilizers. They use rich 12 _____, and other natural elements to return nutrients to the soil.

You might think that since organic produce is grown without using expensive chemicals or large machines, it should, in fact, be less expensive to produce than crops grown with expensive 13 _____. Actually, the opposite is true. This type of farming is very labour-intensive. Farmers need to hire many labourers to remove weeds from their fields the old- fashioned way, with a hand-held hoe rather than with chemicals meant to kill the offending weeds. Because the organic farmers are not adding fertilizer to the soil, they need to 14 _____ the crops and let the land rest periodically. This means that the crop yields are generally lower than those achieved by farmers who use man-made resources to enrich the soil each year.

The next time you walk into a grocery store, ask your- self, "Do I believe all the hype? Is organic produce really better for me?" And if the answer is yes, then look past the occasionally less-attractive 15 _____ of the organic choices and select something healthy to take home— either way, adding more fruits and vegetables to your diet, whether organic or not, is beneficial to your health.

---

(13) *free radical*: molecule with an unpaired elec- tron that reacts easily with other mole- cules and is thought to cause cancer
(16) *pesticides*: chemical mixtures used to kill unwanted plants and insects
(24) *predetermined*: defined in advance
(30) *viability*: continuing productivity
(37) *controversy*: disagreement or argument about something
(39) *tampering*: making changes to something you shouldn't
(43) *supplement*: something added to something else to improve it
(54) *hoe*: garden tool with a long handle and metal blade used to remove weeds
(58) *crop yields*: amount of plants grown

Exercise D

Quiz

"Old wives' tales" are beliefs that are passed down from generation to generation, and they are supposed to provide guidance. Some of these sayings are true and can be helpful, while others are completely false. There are countless "tales" that are related to food. Read the following old wives' tales and indicate if you think they are true (T) or false (F).

☐ 1. You'll get zits (pimples) if you eat too much chocolate or fried food.

☐ 2. Chicken soup is good medicine for a cold.

☐ 3. Wearing a clove of garlic around your neck will prevent you from getting sick.

☐ 4. Putting a steak on a black eye will reduce the swelling.

☐ 5. If you have an upset stomach, you should eat crackers or ginger, or drink flat ginger ale.

☐ 6. Breakfast is the most important meal of the day.

☐ 7. Carrots are good for your eyesight.

☐ 8. Brown eggs are more nutritious than white eggs.

☐ 9. You shouldn't eat between meals—you'll spoil your appetite.

☐ 10. Brown sugar, raw sugar, molasses, and honey are healthier than refined white sugar.

One Step Beyond—Create an Activity

Exercise E

Create an activity similar to Exercise D, using old wives' tales or other stories from your culture.

Grammar Focus

BASE + D/T/N VERBALS

Exercise A

Complete the following sentences using the appropriate verbal form in parentheses.

1. It's a _____ (well-know) fact that many children are enticed to eat junk food by the commercials they see on TV.

2. These _____ (fat-reduce) brownies taste almost as good as the regular ones.

3. We are being advised to eat less _____ (process) food and more organic food.

4. The new healthful eating guidelines _____ (introduce) last year include suggestions for multicultural food choices.

5. The _____ (well-train) diet expert can identify healthy food products at a glance.

6. Although never _____ (prove) by research, people still believe organic food is healthier.

7. The _____ (frequently mention) fact that eating fat makes you fat is really a fallacy.

8. _____ (disappoint) to discover that my favourite sandwich was full of calories, I decided to forgo the butter and mayonnaise.

9. There are many _____ (prepackage) foods on the market that contain organically grown ingredients.

10. Unfortunately, there are many _____ (hide) calories in supposedly healthful foods.

Exercise B

Rewrite the following sentences so that they are more concise.

EXAMPLE: Jean has a cupboard full of fruit that has been canned.

Jean has a cupboard full of **canned** fruit.

1. Top athletes follow diets that have been carefully planned.

_____

_____

2. Fruit which has been organically grown is more expensive.

_____

_____

3. Product placement, which is carefully controlled by marketers, influences our purchases.

_____

_____

4. Produce which is grown locally is seldom sold at your local supermarket.

_____

_____

5. The debate on the benefits of eating organic food, which was televised, was insightful.

_____

_____

6. Food prices, which are carefully controlled, ensure large profits for corporations.

_____

_____

Exercise C

Read the following article about the labelling of organic foods. Underline at least eight examples of base + d/t/n verbals.

Certified Organic

New labelling that was recently introduced in Canada ensures that consumers can now identify genuine organically grown food. Labels now feature the symbol of a maple leaf rising above two hilltops.

5   This labelling indicates that the product has been grown following specific guidelines. For starters, 95 percent of the ingredients contained in the product must be organic. Also, only natural fertilizers can be used in its production. It is important to note that no 10 products can be guaranteed to be completely pesticide-free, even if they are produced organically, because there are so many pollutants in our air and environment. Certified organic livestock needs to be raised in as natural an environment as possible—that means 15 that the animals cannot be kept in tightly packed enclosures or fed food full of additives designed to stimulate rapid growth.

    Now, farmers who want to have their goods labelled as "Canada Organic" must apply to the federally recog- 20 nized certifying board for the privilege. They must submit a detailed report outlining the production methods and the origin of all products that are used in the process.

    A trip to a local supermarket now reveals many "Canada Organic" choices, including fruits, vegetables, 25 cheese, milk, butter, and even some processed foods like cereal and pasta. But as always, buyers should beware. Consumers can be easily fooled by what they may think is equivalent to the organic label. Poultry and eggs may be labelled "free-range." However, free-range 30 products are not necessarily organic. The label could mean that the birds were simply raised in an open pen rather than in the confined spaces that are typical of many large poultry production facilities, but still had chemically enhanced food scattered about for consump- 35 tion. Similarly, customers are often misled by the label "natural." There are no guidelines as to what can be labelled natural—perhaps, to some people, it is natural to inject beef cattle with hormones so they will grow more quickly and reach our tables faster!

40   The organic food industry has increased by significant proportions every year, as more consumers embrace healthful living and attempt to reduce the impact of synthetic chemicals on their lives. This billion-dollar industry is sure to keep expanding as more 45 farmers join the more than 4,000 certified organic growers in Canada.

Exercise D

Complete the following sentences with a base + d/t/n verbal. Use a form of the following base verbs: *simplify, influence, process, standard, concern, utilize, approve, face, establish, clarify*.

1. _____ about misleading labels, Canada has set specific guidelines as to the use of "Canada Organic."

2. Currently, only _____ farmers can sell their products as organic and only _____ products that contain 95 percent certified ingredients can carry the "Canada Organic" label.

3. _____ standards in Canada prevent many products from being labelled as organic when they do not meet the strict guidelines.

4. A _____ definition for the term "organic" will lead to better- _____ consumers.

5. _____ regulations are needed for terms such as "free-range" and "natural."

6. Organic farmers hope that people, _____ by the potential health benefits, will purchase more organic food.

7. Manufacturers, _____ with strict guidelines on the use of the word "organic" will have to change their marketing strategy.

8. Labels, _____ correctly, could help improve the health of many North Americans.

Exercise E

Identify the function of the verbals in Exercise D, such as pre-modifier or post-modifier.

Grammar in Use

Exercise F

Our food choices are influenced by many things, including advertising, availability, amount of time available for food preparation, and cost. With this in mind, complete the following chart.

Category	Food	What influences me to choose that food?
junk food		
fast food		
breakfast		
drink		
dinner		

Now write five sentences describing the results you recorded in the chart.

EXAMPLE: When I'm bored, I eat chips.

Influenced by the catchy commercials, I tried the new flavour of chips.

Vocabulary Expansion

Exercise A

A *suffix* is a group of letters that comes at the end of a word and is joined to the root. Sometimes the suffix adds meaning to the word. At other times, the suffix is used to change the part of speech. Some common suffixes that you may already know are *-ly, -s, ,-less, -ity,* and *–ist.*

Scan through the reading "Supersize Food Invades Japan, but Will it Conquer?" (Student Book, page 146) carefully to find words that contain each of the following suffixes. Complete the chart below by identifying the root word and meaning of each suffix.

One Step Beyond

What other words do you know that end with these suffixes? Find one new word for each suffix and write a sentence showing the meaning of your word.

Exercise B

Reread the article "Certified Organic" on page 98. Circle all the words you find that have the following suffixes: *-ly, -tion, -al, -er.* Insert the words in the chart below and then complete the chart by writing in other forms of the words, where possible.

suffix	noun	verb	adjective	adverb
-ly				
-tion				
-al				
-er				

Exercise C

Complete the following word maps with words formed by adding suffixes to the bases in the circles. Then, write a sentence for each word to show your understanding of the meaning.

EXAMPLE: **select:** selection

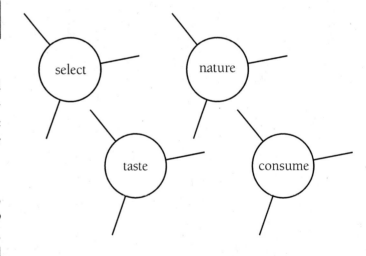

Suffix	Word	Root Word	Meaning or Function of Suffix
-ly			
-ion			
-er			
-al			
-y			
-ful			

One Step Beyond—Create an Activity

Exercise D

Create a matching exercise. Divide your paper into two columns, "Column A" and "Column B." In Column A, list the words you created in Exercise C. In Column B, write definitions for these words in random order. Exchange your work with a classmate and complete each other's activity by matching the words to the definitions.

riting

Body and Concluding Paragraphs

Body Paragraphs

In a five-paragraph essay, the body paragraphs are paragraphs two through four. Each of these paragraphs addresses one aspect of support for the attitude expressed in the thesis. Each paragraph contains a topic sentence that supports the thesis statement and controls the direction of the paragraph. It is very important to link the paragraphs so that the essay is smooth and coherent. This is done through transitional sentences, which are usually the first or last sentence of the paragraph. The exact contents of the body paragraphs will depend on the type of essay being written. The paragraphs should be presented logically, in order of importance, in order of familiarity, or in time order.

Exercise A

One way to determine the topics for the body paragraphs is to turn the thesis statement into a question and then brainstorm possible answers to the question. Each paragraph in the body can address a different answer to the question.

EXAMPLE: **Thesis:** The sales of organic food have increased dramatically in the last few years

> **Question:** Why have the sales of organic food increased dramatically in the last few years?

> **Answers:** a) increased awareness of potential health benefits
> b) more farmers turning to organic farming
> c) organic food is readily available in most supermarkets

Change the following thesis statements into questions and provide three possible answers to each question.

1. **Thesis:** The availability of junk food has changed the traditional eating habits of Japanese youth.

   Question:_____

Answers:

a) _____

b) _____

c) _____

2. **Thesis:** Large food corporations control our food choices.

   Question:_____

   Answers:

   a) _____

   b) _____

   c) _____

3. **Thesis:** Education about healthful living and eating is the key to an improved lifestyle.

   Question:_____

   Answers:

   a) _____

   b) _____

   c) _____

Exercise B

The topic sentence of each paragraph must support one aspect of the thesis statement.

EXAMPLE: **Thesis:** The sales of organic food have increased dramatically in the last few years

Possible topic sentences:

a) Consumers who are concerned about their health are choosing organic food.

b) Many farmers are giving up their pesticides and fertilizers, and following the organic methods of growing food.

c) Catering to an increasing demand, most supermarkets have started selling organic food.

Now rewrite the answers from the three questions in Exercise A into topic sentences.

1. **Thesis:** The availability of junk food has changed the traditional eating habits of Japanese youths.

Topic Sentences:

a) _____

   _____

b) _____

   _____

c) _____

   _____

2. **Thesis:** Large food corporations control our food choices.

Topic Sentences:

a) _____

_____

b) _____

_____

c) _____

_____

3. **Thesis:** Education about healthful living and eating is the key to an improved lifestyle.

Topic Sentences:

a) _____

_____

b) _____

_____

c) _____

_____

Exercise C

Transitional sentences between paragraphs are essential to ensure a smooth, coherent essay. Consider the topic sentences for each thesis statement in Exercise B. Write a transition sentence at the end of paragraph one to connect it to paragraph two. Write another transitional sentence to connect paragraphs two and three.

Thesis: The sales of organic food have increased dramatically in the last few years

Possible Topic Sentences:

1. Consumers who are concerned about their health are choosing organic food.

2. Many farmers are giving up their pesticides and fertilizers, and following the organic methods of growing food.

3. Catering to an increasing demand, most supermarkets have started selling organic food.

EXAMPLE: **Possible transitions:**

a) Healthful food options are increasing as more farmers convert to organic farming.

b) The increased supply of organics has enabled many supermarkets to start offering organic food choices.

1. **Transitions:**

a) _____

_____

b) _____

_____

2. **Transitions:**

a) _____

_____

b) _____

_____

3. **Transitions:**

a) _____

_____

b) _____

_____

Concluding Paragraph

The final paragraph of the essay brings the essay to an end. It contains a reference to, or restatement of, the thesis statement. The final paragraph leaves the reader with some concluding thoughts, but should contain no new information.

Exercise D

Here is a sample concluding paragraph for the following thesis: The sales of organic food have increased dramatically in the last few years.

Conclusion:
Consumption of organically produced food is increasing annually. As more farmers embrace a chemical-free approach to farming, consumers—concerned about the quality of their food—have increased access to healthy organic food. Sales of organic food in supermarkets continue to increase as informed consumers put a premium on eating healthily.

Write sample conclusions for the three outlines you developed in Exercise B.

Exercise E

Write an essay based on one of the outlines you developed in Exercise B, or on a topic of your choice. Use the checklists on the following page to edit your work.

☑ Body Paragraph Checklist

☐ Does each paragraph have a topic sentence that supports one aspect of my thesis statement?

☐ Does the information in each paragraph support my topic sentence?

☐ Does each paragraph contain a transitional sentence?

☐ Do my paragraphs contain sentences that are grammatically correct?

☑ Concluding Paragraph Checklist

☐ Does my paragraph restate, summarize, or refer to my thesis statement?

☐ Have I avoided introducing any new ideas in this paragraph?

☐ Have I left my reader with something to think about?

Academic Word List

acquisition	design	pursue
categories	expansion	range
conduct	layer	shift
consumer	location	stress
corporate	percent	technology
data	process	trend
decline	purchase	

Exercise A
Word Meaning

Circle the word in parentheses that matches each of the following definitions.

1. groups of things with similar features (acquisition / categories / conduct)

2. information, especially facts or numbers (range / data / percent)

3. a thin sheet of a substance (layer / location / principle)

4. worry caused by a difficult situation (purchase / pursue / stress)

5. a general development in the way people are behaving (technology / trend / purchase)

6. the way in which something is planned or made (layer / design / data)

7. a downward movement, gradual loss (decline / expansion / percent)

8. a method of producing goods (process / range / trend)

9. goods of one particular type sold in a shop (categories / expansion / range)

10. a change from one place or position to another (trend / shift / percent)

11. to buy (purchase / design / shift)

12. an increase in size (location / process / expansion)

13. relating to a large company (design / corporate / consumer)

14. industrial discoveries (technology / expansion / range)

15. a person who buys goods or services for their own use (purchase / corporate / consumer)

16. an amount of something expressed out of 100 (percent / design / data)

17. a place or position (layer / trend / location)

18. something obtained (acquisition / categories / expansion)

19. to try to achieve something (design / decline / pursue)

20. to carry out (decline / conduct / design)

Exercise B
Pronunciation—Syllables and Stress

Listen to your teacher or an audio dictionary to hear the pronunciation for each word in the list. Repeat each word aloud. Mark the syllables and major word stress.

1. acquisition (n): ac / qui / s i / tion

2. categories (n): _____

3. conduct (n): _____

4. consumer (n): _____

5. corporate (adj): _____

6. data (n): _____

7. decline (n): _____

8. design (n): _____

9. expansion (n): _____

10. layer (n): _____

11. location (n): _____

12. percent (n): _____

13. process (n): _____

14. purchase (v): _____

15. pursue (v): _____

16. range (n): _____

17. shift (n): _____

18. stress (n): _____

19. technology (n): _____

20. trend (n): _____

Exercise C

Word Forms

Fill in each blank with the word form indicated in parentheses. More than one word may be possible for each indicated word form.

1. acquisition (n): _____ (v)
   _____ (adj)

2. categories (n): _____ (v)

3. conduct (n): _____ (v)

4. consumer (n): _____ (v)
   _____ (adj)

5. corporate (adj): _____ (n)

6. decline (n): _____ (adj)

7. design (n): _____ (v)

8. expansion (n): _____ (v)
   _____ (adj)

9. layer (n): _____ (adj)

10. location (n): _____ (v)

11. percent (n): _____ (n)

12. process (n): _____ (v)
    _____ (adj)

13. purchase (v): _____ (adj)

14. pursue (v): _____ (n)
    _____ (adj)

15. shift (n): _____ (adj)

16. stress (n): _____ (adj)

17. technology (n): _____ (adj)
    _____ (adv)

18. trend (n): _____ (adj)

Exercise D

In a dictionary, find one example sentence for each circled word in Exercise A and copy it into your notebook. Draft a second sentence of your own. Then, work with a partner to revise and edit your sentence.

Exercise E

Read the following story and complete each blank with one of the words from the list. You do not have to change the grammatical form of any of the words. Use each word only once.

acquire	decline	purchased
conduct	design	shifts
consumer	expanding	technology
corporations	locate	trends
data		

1 _____ spend billions of dollars trying to persuade the 2 _____ to purchase their products. They keep a keen eye on market 3 _____, looking for evidence of any 4 _____ in buying patterns that indicate whether their sales will potentially 5 _____ or if they should be 6 _____ their product line. The corporations hire marketing consultants to 7 _____ focus groups with consumers in order to 8 _____ the consumers' opinions on the products that they have 9 _____ recently. Corporations also use 10 _____ to track people's purchases. Every time a bar code is swiped in a store, the sale of each product is recorded. The corporations then use this 11 _____ to inform their marketing plans. Included in these marketing plans are the special fees that corporations pay grocery stores to 12 _____ their products at eye level of the consumer—a location proven to increase sales. The 13 _____ of the supermarket is carefully planned to encourage consumers to purchase more products.

categorized	processed	range
layered	pursue	stress
percentage		

Fast food is often 14 _____ as junk food. A typical hamburger 15 _____ with a slice of 16 _____ cheese contains over 500 calories. It is recommended that an average-sized adult consume between 1500 and 2000 calories a day. In principle, a large 17 _____ of these calories should come from healthy food, not junk food—so eating at fast food restaurants regularly is not a good idea. Health organizations 18 _____ that we should include a 19 _____ of foods in our diets, including lean proteins, some carbohydrates and a limited amount of fat. In order to help ourselves 20 _____ a healthy lifestyle, we should remain mindful of the impact that junk food can have on our health.

Unit 10
The Circle of Life

Vocabulary

Exercise A

Let's play a word game! The definitions below correspond to ten of the vocabulary words in the box. Ask the question "What is?" about each word from the list as you match it to a definition.

EXAMPLE: This five-syllable word is synonymous with "sequential" when used as an adjective.

"What is chronological?"

adolescent	identity	puberty
baby boomers	life coach	retirement
chronological	longevity	revolutionize
decade	mature	stage
fertile		

1.   This is the time in a person's life when they are no longer working because they have reached an older age.
     What is _____ (noun)?

2.   This is a period of ten years.
     What is a _____ (noun)?

3.   This word means a period of development. What is a _____ (noun)?

4.   If you ask people to describe themselves, they will talk about their personality traits, their age, the groups they belong to, the things they like and dislike, and so on. These personal descriptions are considered a person's _____ .
     What is an _____ (noun)?

5.   This word refers to a person who is no longer a child but is not yet an adult.
     What is an _____ (noun)?

6.   This word emphasizes the physical and emotional changes that occur during the time period when a child becomes a teenager.
     What is _____ (noun)?

7.   You'll find this word about three-quarters of the way through any dictionary. You can use the verb form in the sentence, "The Internet has _____ how people communicate" to describe the fast and complete change the Internet has caused. In its noun form, it is commonly used to describe a significant and fast political change such as the French _____ or the Russian _____.
     What is _____ (base verb)?

8.   A high-school or post-secondary student who is older than the usual age is referred to as this type of student. If you still can't guess the word, remember that girls do this faster than boys. What is _____ (base verb)?

9.   The word describes someone or something that is able to have a baby.
     What is _____ (adjective)?

10.   This word is synonymous with "long life expectancy".
      What is _____ (noun)?

Now use each word in a sentence that demonstrates your comprehension of its meaning.

Exercise B

Many of the words above are used to describe the human life cycle. The words can be used in other situations as well. Use a thesaurus, dictionary, or other source to discover at least three synonyms (or synonymous phrases) for each of the following words: *stage*, *longevity*, *revolutionize*, *mature*, *fertile*. Write sentences, using the words you discover, on a separate sheet of paper.

EXAMPLE: **chronological:** in order of time; sequential, historical

The child told his parents everything he did at camp that week sequentially from when they dropped him off until when they picked him up.

Exercise C

Read an English newspaper or magazine and look for the following words (or a form of these words): *decade*, *revolutionary*, *longevity*, *maturity*. Write out the sentence that contains each word and be prepared to explain the context of the sentence. You're likely to find these words in articles about business, politics, or technology.

Grammar Focus

TENSE REVIEW

Exercise A

Some of the underlined verbs in the sentences below are in the correct tense, and some are not. Write C for correct or I for incorrect, and correct the inaccuracies.

Note: Let the meaning and the tenses of other verbs in the sentence guide you.

☐ 1. Psychologists agree that age <u>played</u> an important role in how people interact with each other.

☐ 2. The stage of human development called "youth" only <u>will take on</u> its current meaning a few decades ago.

☐ 3. The "Ages-and-Stages" approach to adult development <u>had been criticized</u> because it doesn't appear to apply to women.

☐ 4. In the future, advertisers <u>have no longer targeted</u> the youth market.

☐ 5. Before the US army changed its rules in 2005, the maximum enlistment age for active duty in the army <u>had been</u> 35.

☐ 6. These days, by the time many couples get married, they <u>will likely live</u> together for at least one year.

☐ 7. People commonly believe that intellectual abilities slowly <u>deteriorated</u> with advancing age.

☐ 8. Nowadays, people <u>live longer and stay</u> healthy into their 70s and 80s.

Exercise B

Fill in the blanks with the correct tense of the verb *develop*. Try to use each tense only once.

1. Children _____ language skills very early.

2. During the 1960s, North American teens—without realizing it— _____ a new social system for young adults that would last into the next thirty years and beyond.

3. For about a year now, engineers at Alpha Computers _____ a new virtual software program that allows users to project themselves into the future.

4. Researchers _____ (just develop) an early detection system for this genetic disorder.

5. Now, at 24, Martha _____ an interest in children.

6. In the early part of the 20th century, the famous Swiss psychologist, Jean Piaget, _____ a comprehensive theory about human development, but it ignored adult development entirely.

7. I am certain that we _____ new ways to combat age-related diseases during the next decade.

8. Many people believe that by the middle of the 21st century, scientists _____ a system for extending life into the 100-year range or beyond.

9. As you get older, you _____ memory loss.

10. The Canadian pharmaceutical industry _____ (already develop) a new drug for colon cancer when Pharma AGF in Germany announced its new cancer-fighting drug.

Exercise C

Write sentences using the following verbs in the tenses indicated in parentheses.

1. retire (future continuous)
   _____

2. identify (future simple)
   _____

3. develop (past continuous)
   _____

4. mature (present perfect continuous)
   _____

5. coach (present continuous)
   _____

6. span (present simple
   _____

7. identify (future perfect)
   _____

8. mature (past simple)
   _____

9. expect (past perfect)
   _____

10. give (future perfect continuous)
    _____

11. revolutionize (present perfect)
    _____

12. expect (past perfect continuous)
    _____

Vocabulary Expansion

Exercise A
Word Intimacy

The word "cover," when used as a verb, can indicate the range of protection offered by insurance. As a noun, "coverage" can be used to mean financial protection in case something bad happens. As an adjective, "covered" can mean something that is protected by insurance.

Look up the word "cover" in the dictionary and write a sentence for each of its different uses. Note that "cover" is often associated with specific words, such as the prepositions and verbs in the examples below.

EXAMPLES: to be covered by
to cover someone for / against
to arrange coverage of / for

Now choose two or three words from the reading "No Age Limit On Stages Of Life" on page 162 of your Student Book, (such as *stages*, *policies*, *impact*, *limit*, or *opportunity*) and use a dictionary to analyze the functions, meanings, and word associations of these words.

For each word

1. list its meanings and write a sentence for each meaning.

2. list other grammatical forms and their meanings if they differ from the meanings in point one.

3. list other words often associated with it.

Be prepared to share your work with your classmates.

Exercise B

Match the prepositions in the following box with the nouns in the oval. Note that in some cases more than one preposition can be used with each noun.

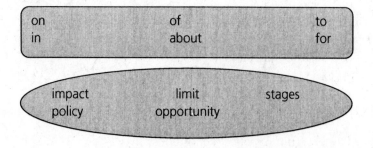

| on | of | to |
| in | about | for |

impact · limit · stages
policy · opportunity

Write a sentence for each noun + preposition combination.

One Step Beyond — Create An Activity
Exercise C

Design a word game activity like the one in Vocabulary 1, Exercise A in this unit. Choose ten words from Reading 2, pages 162 to 164 in your Student Book. Write clues and then exchange your activity with a classmate.

Grammar Expansion

Shifting Tenses

You will notice in the reading "The Cardboard Box Is Marked 'The Good Stuff'" (in the Student Book, pages 156 to 157) that although we can identify a main time perspective for each paragraph, there are occasional shifts in time, and consequently shifts in tense. Normally, it is not acceptable in English to shift tenses unnecessarily. However, there are situations when it is acceptable.

It is acceptable to shift tenses when

1. *you are giving specific examples to illustrate a general statement.*

   Driven by a desire to understand human nature, physicians, philosophers, and other professionals have critically examined the motivations, challenges, and key influences in human behaviour at various key stages of human development. Critical work in this field was done at the turn of the 19th century by Sigmund Freud, a trained physician, who theorized that children's development could be defined in terms of psychosexual development.

2. *you are showing an important and clearly signalled contrast in time.*

   Many North American parents and educators continually praise children's work because they believe that high self-esteem leads to better learning and greater success. But a recent study revealed that children who believed they were extremely clever actually did worse on tests they could easily have passed because they simply did not try hard. The children not only chose easy tests that they knew they could score high on, they rated effort as something reserved for hopeless students. According to the study's author, children who identify with statements such as "I always try hard" and "I don't give up" achieve more and do better regardless of their natural ability. This suggests that parents and educators would do better to teach children the value of hard work than to praise unnecessarily.

3. *you are interrupting your text with a statement of general truth.*

Grandmother didn't want to enter the nursing home, despite Mother's urging. Sadly, Grandmother could no longer prepare her own meals or even wash herself. My mother, my sisters, and I took turns cleaning and cooking for Grandmother, but this was becoming increasingly stressful for our own families. Nonetheless, Grandmother simply wouldn't hear of going into a nursing home. She said that as long as she was in her own home, she had some sense of being in control. People want to be in control of their own lives—that's only natural. Grandmother finally did enter the home, but not until two years later. And those were two years she cherished.

Exercise A

In the three example paragraphs, underline the sentences or clauses that show a change in time perspective.

Exercise B

Helen attended a reunion of some of her colleagues from the tourism board where she worked ten years ago. Read the thank-you note she wrote to her host. Rewrite the note, putting a form of each verb in parentheses in an appropriate tense. (You may have to supply modals in some cases to make the meaning clear.)

Dear Barbara,

It 1 _____ (be) great to see you and the gang at the reunion last Saturday. Thanks for inviting me. I 2 _____ (not believe) how time 3 _____ (fly)!

The last time I 4 _____ (see) Cathy and Bernhardt, they 5 _____ (have) no children. Now they 6 _____ (be) the parents of three adorable little ones. Deborah 7 _____ (not look) a day older than when I 8 _____ (see) her ten years ago. And Ava and Steve's two children 9 _____ (look) so grown up. 10 _____ (Be) Jessica really only eleven? She 11 _____ (look) like such a young lady. It 12 _____ (seem) that only yesterday Ava 13 _____ (announce) she 14 _____ (be) pregnant with Philip. Truly, where 15 _____ (go, the time)? It 16 _____ (be) great to see everyone's photos too — Karen's son Shaun with the gold medal he 17 _____ (win) for snowboarding, and Jamie speed skiing. Those boys 18 _____ (be) Olympic medallists one day. 19 _____ (you believe) that Dave's daughter 20 _____ (marry) last year? She 21 _____ (be) just a child when we 22 _____ (work) at the tourist board. Before you know it our own children 23 _____ (marry) and 24 _____ (leave) the nest. Hope to see you all again before then. Thanks again for the great time.

Love,
Helen, Mike, Jacklyn, and Paul

Exercise C

Aesop's Fables are loved by millions of North American children. Read "The Town Mouse and the Country Mouse," and fill in the blanks with an appropriate forms of the verbs in parentheses. Look carefully at the context when deciding on the appropriate tense of each verb. (Tenses may change in some situations.)

The Town Mouse and the Country Mouse

A country mouse 1 _____ (be) very happy that his city cousin, the town mouse, 2 _____ (accept) his invitation to dinner. He 3 _____ (give) his city cousin all the best food he 4 _____ (have), such as dried beans, peas, and crusts of bread. The town mouse 5 _____ (try) not to show how he 6 _____ (dislike) the food and 7 _____ (pick) a little here and 8 _____ (taste) a little there to be polite. After dinner, however, he 9 _____ (say), "How can you 10 _____ (stand) such food all the time? Still I 11 _____ (suppose) here in the country you 12 _____ (not know) about any better. Why 13 _____ (you not go) home with me?

Once you 14 _____ (taste) the delicious things I 15 _____ (eat), you 16 _____ (never want) to come back here." The country mouse not only kindly 17 _____ (forgive) the town mouse for not liking his dinner, but even 18 _____ (consent) to go that very evening to the city with his cousin. They 19 _____ (arrive) late at night, and the city mouse, as host, 20 _____ (take) his country cousin at once to a room where there 21 _____ (be) a big dinner. "You 22 _____ (must be) tired," he 23 _____ (say). "24 _____ (rest) here, and I 25 _____ (bring) you some real food." And he 26 _____ (bring) the country mouse such things as nuts, dates, cakes, and fruit. The country mouse 27 _____ (think) it was all so good, he 28 _____ (want) to stay there. But before he 29 _____ (have) a chance to say so, he 30 _____ (hear) a terrible roar, and looking up, he 31 _____ (see) a huge creature dash into the room. Frightened half out of his wits, the country mouse 32 _____ (run) from the table, and round and round the room, trying to find a hiding place. At last he

33 _____ (find) a place of safety. While he 34 _____ (stand) there trembling, he 35 _____ (make) up his mind to go home as soon as he 36 _____ (can get) safely away; for, to himself, he 37 _____ (say) "I'd rather 38 _____ (have) common food in safety than dates and nuts in the midst of danger."

The troubles you know 39 _____ (be) the easiest to bear.

Grammar In Use

Exercise D

Write a letter to an English-speaking Canadian friend, describing how young people in your native country or region like to spend their school holidays. Give a specific personal example of such a holiday.

One Step Beyond—Create an Activity

Exercise E

Choose a paragraph from a newspaper, magazine, or novel. Copy the paragraph onto a page, replacing each verb in the text with its simple infinitive (verb without "to") in parentheses. Exchange your activity with a classmate and write each simple infinitive verb in an appropriate tense.

Writing

Narrative and Descriptive Essays

Narrative Essays

The narrative essay, like the narrative paragraph, tells a story. The events can be real or fictional, but the story must illustrate a point the writer is making. The paragraphs should be arranged logically in a chronological order.

Exercise A

Reread "The Town Mouse and The Country Mouse" on pages 107/108 and divide the story into eight main events. List the events in the order that they happen.

1. _____

2. _____

3. _____

4. _____

5. _____

6. _____

7. _____

8. _____

Descriptive Essays

The descriptive essay, like the descriptive paragraph, describes a person, a place, an object, or an event in great detail so that the reader can clearly picture what is being described. An essay is used in preference to a paragraph when the topic is somewhat complex and would benefit from a lengthier, fuller, more detailed description.

Exercise B

Find a colour photo in a magazine (perhaps a vacation spot in a travel magazine) of a place that you find interesting. Look at the photo and imagine that you are in the location pictured. Under each of the senses listed below, write precise descriptive words or phrases to describe what you experience when you are there.

Your reader will get a much clearer mental picture of your description if you include detailed sensory images. Brainstorming sensory images is useful at the outline stage.

sight: _____

_____

_____

sound: _____

_____

_____

smell: _____

_____

_____

taste: _____

_____

_____

physical feelings: _____
_____
_____

emotional feelings: _____
_____
_____

Exercise C

Write about one of the following topics. Use the Essay Checklists that follow this exercise to edit your work.

1. Using the six pictures in the illustration below as a guide, write a narrative essay (fable) about a merchant, his son, and a donkey. Remember to include your main point in your introduction.

2. Write a narrative essay about a special childhood memory and explain why the event was special.

3. Interview an older relative and write a narrative essay about that person's life.

4. Write a descriptive essay about someone who is much younger than you are, or someone much older. Describe the person's appearance, character, and behaviours.

5. Write a descriptive essay. Describe, in detail, one of the following places:

   a) a crowded shopping mall

   b) your grandparents' house or apartment

   c) an airport terminal

   d) a children's playground

☑ Essay Checklists

Outline

- ☐ Did I brainstorm ideas?
- ☐ Have I identified my audience?
- ☐ Does my essay have a title?
- ☐ Is my topic sufficiently narrowed?
- ☐ Have I eliminated ideas that don't relate?
- ☐ Does my thesis statement contain a controlling idea (attitude)?
- ☐ Do the topic sentences in the body support my thesis?
- ☐ Do I have at least two to three points to illustrate the main point made in each of my topic sentences?

Introductory Paragraph

- ☐ Will my paragraph get the reader's attention?
- ☐ Does my paragraph contain a thesis statement which indicates my point of view?
- ☐ Does my paragraph use one of the four main approaches: attention grabber, quotation, opposite, or cone?
- ☐ Does my introductory paragraph provide some background information?
- ☐ Does my introductory paragraph indicate the kind of essay that I will develop?

Body Paragraphs

- ☐ Does each paragraph have a topic sentence that supports one aspect of my thesis statement?
- ☐ Does the information in each paragraph support my topic sentence?
- ☐ Does each paragraph contain a transitional sentence?
- ☐ Do my paragraphs contain sentences that are grammatically correct?

Concluding Paragraph

- ☐ Does my paragraph restate, summarize, or refer to my thesis statement?
- ☐ Have I avoided introducing any new ideas in this paragraph?
- ☐ Have I left my reader with something to think about?

Editing

- ☐ Are my essay's sentences and ideas arranged logically?
- ☐ Have I used transitional expressions adequately and appropriately?
- ☐ Have I checked my essay to make sure the meaning of each sentence is clear?
- ☐ Have I checked my essay to make sure that I have used precise words and the correct form of words?
- ☐ Have I proofread my essay for errors in grammar, punctuation, and spelling?

Academic Word List

administration	environment	policy
attitudes	identified	principal
available	impact	psychology
commission	institute	series
conference	maximum	significant
contract	participation	similar
definition	period	

Exercise A
Word Meaning

Replace each of the following underlined words or phrases with a synonym from the choices provided.

1. The <u>effect</u> of a healthy lifestyle on longevity is well-known.

   identification   impact   period

2. The government <u>requested</u> a study on life expectancy.

   participation   principle   commissioned

3. Early stimulation of a child's brain has <u>considerable</u> effects on later intellectual development.

    significant   similar   available

4. All the <u>people</u> in the research study were elderly.

    principal   administration   participants

5. The <u>description</u> of adulthood has been changing.

    attitude   institution   definition

6. People's <u>mental</u> health is just as important as their physical health.

    psychological   environmental   attitude

7. The army changed its <u>formal rule</u> regarding the maximum enlistment age.

    administration   policy   institute

8. The student government at the college held a <u>meeting</u> for all students to discuss tuition hikes.

    commission   policy   conference

9. The new <u>governing group</u> changed its foreign policy.

    administration   contract   series

10. The book was not <u>accessible</u> in the library because someone had borrowed it.

    identified   significant   available

11. Children in middle school today experience <u>surroundings</u> much more like what their parents experienced in high school.

    attitudes   environments   administrations

12. A positive <u>mindset</u> in life may improve longevity.

    series   definition   attitude

13. Chris signed an <u>agreement</u> with the company to work in its Tokyo office for two years.

    contract   policy   commission

14. The <u>school leader</u> introduced a new arts program into the school.

    commission   principal   conference

15. She <u>described</u> herself as Canadian.

    identified   maximize   participate

16. The <u>order</u> of events that led to her decision was unusual.

    institution   series   policies

17. The NIA is an <u>organization</u> that studies aging.

    policy   institution   administration

18. The <u>highest</u> number of students who can enroll in the course is 35.

    similar   series   maximum

19. The <u>stage</u> of young adulthood lasts longer today than it did a few decades ago.

    definition   environment   period

20. Although children today are different in many ways from children 30 years ago, in some ways they are <u>alike</u>.

    available   identified   similar

Exercise B
Pronunciation—Syllables and Stress

Listen to your teacher or an audio dictionary to hear the pronunciation for each word in the list. Repeat each word aloud. Mark the syllables and major word stress.

1. administration (n): ad / min / i / **stra** / tion
2. attitudes (n): _____
3. available (adj): _____
4. commission (n): _____
5. conference (n): _____
6. contract (n): _____
7. definition (n): _____
8. environment (n): _____
9. identified (adj): _____
10. impact (n): _____
11. institute (n): _____
12. maximum (adj): _____
13. participation (n): _____
14. period (n): _____
15. policy (n): _____
16. principal (n): _____
17. psychology (n): _____
18. series (n): _____
19. significant (adj): _____
20. similar (adj): _____

Exercise C
Word Forms

Fill in each blank with the word form indicated in parentheses. More than one word may be possible for each indicated word form.

1. administration (n): _____ (v)
   _____ (adj) _____ (adv)

2. available (adj): _____ (n)

3. commission (n): _____ (v)
   _____ (adj)

4. conference (n): _____ (v)
   _____ (adj)

5. contract (n): _____ (n)
   _____ (adj)

6. definition (n): _____ (v)

7. environment (n): _____ (adj)
   _____ (adv)

8. identified (v): _____ (n)
   _____ (adj)

9. impact (n): _____ (v)
   _____ (adj)

10. institute (n): _____ (n)
    _____ (adj)

11. maximum (adj): _____ (v)

12. participation (n): _____ (v)
    _____ (adj)

13. period (n): _____ (adj)
    _____ (adv)

14. psychology (n): _____ (adj)
    _____ (adv)

15. series (n): _____ (adj)

16. significant (adj): _____ (n)
    _____ (adv)

17. similar (adj): _____ (n)
    _____ (adv)

Exercise D

In a dictionary, find two example sentences for each word in Exercise A and copy them into your notebook. Draft a third sentence of your own. Then, work with a partner to revise and edit your sentences.

Exercise E

Read the following story and complete each blank with one of the words from the list. You do not have to change the grammatical form of any of the words. Use each word only once.

> attitudes   defined   psychology
> commissioned institutes   significant

Stages of life are not $_1$ _____ in the same way they used to be. There has been a $_2$ _____ shift in $_3$ _____ towards aging. The age of 65 used to be considered old, but today many people can expect to enjoy a healthy, active life at 65. Various government and health $_4$ _____ have $_5$ _____ research studies on aging. The results of many studies suggest that the $_6$ _____ of aging is changing.

> environments   principal   similar
> policies

Many adolescents in North America are growing up in $_7$ _____ that are $_8$ _____ to what their parents experienced at a much later age. For example, children date at an earlier age than their parents did, they "graduate" from kindergarten, and their social networks have increased dramatically. Martine Reiss, a middle school $_9$ _____, says that society is dealing with a new kind of youth. She says that schools have had to adjust their $_{10}$ _____ to respond to this new reality. For example, Reiss has introduced supervised school dances on a monthly basis. Previously, there had been a rule that the school would not hold dances.

> administrators maximum   period
> contracts   participation series
> impact

Shifts in attitudes about age are not only found among youth. Baby boomers, who have now entered the 50-plus age group, have redefined what age range is now considered elderly. With increased life expectancy, the $_{11}$ _____ of adulthood has been extended beyond age 65, and once again society is responding accordingly. Government and company $_{12}$ _____ understand the $_{13}$ _____ of redefining adulthood and old age to their business and the economy generally. They are adjusting health and employment policies to reflect the extended $_{14}$ _____ of older adults in the workforce. For example, the mandatory retirement age of 65 has been changed, so that in many companies, workers can work longer. In the US army, the

15 _____ enlistment age has been increased from 35 to 42. Many health insurance companies have implemented a 16 _____ of changes to their health insurance policies as well. Some health insurance companies now provide 17 _____ that insure children of beneficiaries up to age 30.

| available | conferences | identified |

With increased longevity and an aging population, aging has become a national obsession. The number of articles on aging, the amount of money spent on aging research, and the numerous 18 _____ on aging being organized across North America illustrate the importance of the shift in how we view the stages of life. More than 3,500 professionals from the fields of aging, healthcare, and education, as well as business leaders, attended the 2008 conference on Aging in America to learn, network and discuss the issues of aging. Whatever issues have been 19 _____, one thing remains clear: older adults have many more opportunities 20 _____ today for leading healthy, active lives than they did just a few decades ago.

Answer Key

Unit 1

Vocabulary

Exercise A

1. The snow was blinding, so we pulled off the road.
2. At 10:45 p.m. last night, the volcano erupted.
3. A twister touched down and destroyed everything in its path.
4. The earthquake caused great fissures.
5. The volcano emitted poisonous gases.
6. The epicentre of the earthquake was the coast of Los Angeles.
7. The aftershocks were strong enough to rattle the dishes.
8. The eye of the hurricane is calm and quiet.

Exercise B

1. infrastructure
2. cyclic
3. devastated
4. preparation
5. drought
6. factor
7. degradation
8. phenomenon
9. substandard
10. vulnerability

Vocabulary Expansion 1

Exercise C

strong
light } breeze
pleasant

freezing
driving
pouring
spitting
drizzling } rain
pelting
light
heavy

blinding
freezing
driving
pelting
powdery } snow
light
granular
packing
heavy

strong
gale-force
light } wind
north-easterly

Exercise D

1. mist, spitting, drizzle, downpour
2. light, powdery, packing, heavy, blinding
3. light, high, strong, gale-force

Grammar Focus 1

Exercise A

1. Predictions of impending doom have been issued for the past few years by scientists who study the earth's atmosphere.
2. Global warming has been caused by a rise in carbon emissions.
3. Statements were made by individual researchers that human activity has contributed to global warming.
4. Drastic steps must be taken by the world to reduce the emissions of heat-trapping gases.
5. Huge tracts of densely-populated land will be flooded by rising oceans.
6. The effects of carbon dioxide emissions, methane, and chlorofluorocarbons are simulated by complex computers.

Exercise B

1. Aerosols which cool the planet by blocking the sun can mask the effects of global warming.
2. Water from melting glaciers will submerge many beaches.
3. Global warming will affect temperature and rainfall patterns.
4. Deep ocean currents influence our world climate.
5. We must reduce emissions to the same levels as in the 1920s.
6. Industrialized nations must take the lead role in reducing global warming.

Exercise C

1. description: performer not important
2. description: performer not important or to emphasize the receiver of the action not the performer
3. description: performer not important or to emphasize the receiver of the action not the performer
4. authoritative tone
5. emphasize receiver of action
6. description: performer not important

Exercise D

1. performer: scientists; delete (sometimes the performer is left in to emphasize source)
2. performer: David Suzuki; not possible to delete
3. performer: people; delete

4. performer: scientists; delete
    (sometimes the performer is left in to emphasize source)
5. performer: humans; delete

Exercise E

Possible answers:
1. Public building
2. Hospital or any public building
3. Farm or other large, privately-owned property
4. Mall or other public washroom
5. Insurance contract

Vocabulary Expansion 2

Exercise A

1. c
2. e
3. b
4. d
5. a

Exercise B

Possible answers:

1. It's raining very hard.
2. She left him penniless.
3. Lucas misled his mother.
4. She likes to sit around and chat with her co-workers.
5. We had to give up our hope of owning a house.
6. I want to go to bed early tonight.
7. Habib risked everything to start his new business.
8. I'll accept that invitation at a future time.

Grammar Focus 2

Exercise A

Tenses (sentences will vary):

1. simple past — was / were recorded
2. simple present — am / is / are controlled
3. present continuous — am / is being destroyed
4. past continuous — was / were being ignored
5. present perfect — has been observed
6. past perfect — had been decided
7. future — will be developed

Exercise B

1. A myth about a beautiful maiden was created by a First Nations tribe from Niagara to explain the origin of Horseshoe Falls.
2. The earth was divided into several parts, separated by many great lakes by the sun.
3. Ayers Rock is considered a spiritual place by the Aboriginal people of Australia.
4. Blocks were carved out of snow by the Inuit to build igloos.
5. The weather is controlled by powerful spirits.

Exercise C

1. is
2. be taught
3. become
4. makes
5. be
6. be developed and studied
7. unlearn
8. be taken
9. be embraced

Exercise D

1. *Separate all recyclables from your garbage.*
2. Turn off the lights.
3. Use compact fluorescent bulbs.
4. Unplug all electronics not in use.
5. Use public transportation.
6. Replace old appliances in your home.

Grammar Expansion

Exercise E

1. gets / is
2. gets / is
3. got / was
4. was
5. got / was

Exercises F and G

Answers will vary.

Writing

Exercise A

1. The economic damage is still being calculated
2. Farmers lost a lifetime of work
3. The army played a key role
4. Volunteers helped in any way they could

Exercise B

2 and 5

Exercise C

1. first sentence
2. last sentence

Exercise D

Answers will vary.

Exercise A
Word Meaning

1. element
2. factors
3. proportions
4. community
5. research
6. adequate
7. variable
8. complex
9. reject
10. funds
11. affect
12. major
13. estimate
14. consequences
15. generate
16. region
17. area
18. potential
19. cycle
20. issues

Exercise B

1. **ǎd** / e / quate
2. af / **fěct**
3. **ǎ** / re / a
4. com / **mǔn** / i / ty
5. com / **plěx**
6. **cǒn** / se / quen / ces
7. **cў** / cle
8. **ě** / le /ments
9. **ěs** / ti / mate
10. **fǎc** / tors
11. **fǔnds**
12. **gěn** / er / a / ted
13. **ǐs** / sues
14. **mǎ** / jor
15. po / **těn** / tial
16. pro / **pǒr** / tions
17. **rě** / gion
18. re / **jěc** / ted
19. **rě** / search
20. **vǎr** / i / a / ble

Exercise C

1. (adv) adequately
2. (adj) affective   (adv) affectively
3. (n) complexity
4. (adj) consequent   (adv) consequently
5. (adj) cyclical
6. (adj) elemental
7. (n) estimation   (adj) estimated
8. (v) factor
9. (n) funders / funding
10. (n) generation
11. (n) majority /major
12. (adj) potential   (adv) potentially
13. (adj) (dis)proportionate / (dis)proportioned
    (adv) (dis)proportionally
14. (adj) regional   (adv) regionally
15. (n) rejection
16. (n) researcher
17. (n) variation   (v) vary

Exercise D

Answers will vary.

Exercise E

1. adequately
2. cyclical
3. areas
4. affected
5. potential
6. communities
7. consequently
8. Researchers
9. factors
10. major
11. complex
12. estimate
13. variable
14. elements
15. regions
16. disproportionate
17. issues
18. funding
19. generate
20. reject

Unit 2

Vocabulary

Exercise A

1. psychic
2. astrology
3. numerology
4. clairvoyance / telepathy
5. telepathy / clairvoyance
6. subconscious
7. Reincarnation

Exercise B

Across
1. levitate
2. omens
3. curse
4. voodoo
5. apparitions
6. psychokinetic
7. medium
8. seance

Down
1. poltergeist
2. telepathy
3. shaman
4. premonitions

Exercise C

Answers will vary.

Vocabulary Expansion

Exercise A

1. posthypnotic: after hypnosis
   posthumously: after death
   post- = after, behind, following

2. demystify: take away the mystery
   demean: cause reduction in respect for someone
   de- = reduce, from, away, off

3. transcend: go beyond
   transmit: send through
   trans- = through, beyond

4. monotheistic: believing in one god
   monotonous: dull and never changing
   (from monotone: a single sound that never varies)
   mono- = one, alone

5. dissatisfied: not satisfied
   discredited: not respected anymore
   dis- = apart from, separate, loss of, not

6. malediction: curse (words meant to bring harm)
   malicious: bad, harmful
   mal- = bad, wrong

Exercise B

Answers will vary.

Exercise C

Possible answers:

decaffeinated, decode, deformed, deport

disarrange, disreputable, disfigure, dishonest, disagree

malformed, maladjusted

monogram

parapsychology, paraphrase

postsecondary, postscript

prearrange, premature, preview, prefigure

subheading, subhuman

superhuman, supernova, superscript

rearrange, review, reformed, readjusted, report, replant, rephrase

telegram, telemarketing

transmission, transcript, transport, transplant

Grammar Focus 1

Exercise A

Answers may vary according to the interpretation of the context in which these statements were made.

1. Ms. H. admitted that a few ghosts from her past had come back to haunt her.

   Ms. H. admitted that a few ghosts from her past have come back to haunt her.

2. Mr. B. said that there had been many unexplained events in that government last year.

3. Mr. J. was overheard saying that he believed the leader had been a fox in his previous life.

4. Mr. M. predicted that his party would balance the budget this year.

5. Mr. P. assured voters that he was learning to speak a second language because he had discovered that being monolingual in a bilingual country was a curse.

6. Mr. J. announced that he envisions a country his children and grandchildren could be proud of.

   Mr. J. announced that he envisioned a country his children and grandchildren could be proud of.

7. Mr. L. said that one didn't have to be a psychic to know that governing a bilingual country would continue to be a challenge in the future.

   Mr. L. said that one doesn't have to be a psychic to know that governing a bilingual country will continue to be a challenge in the future.

Exercise B

Possible answers:

Jerome Harrold: "Dr. Marilyn Boch reported seeing a spaceship-like object at about 10:15 p.m. on Tuesday night."

Jerome Harrold: "I am sceptical about the sighting despite the photographs."

Jerome Harrold: "Perhaps Dr. Boch has been watching too many episodes of *Unsolved Mysteries*."

Jerome Harrold: "The Academy will hold a complete investigation into the sighting."

Dr. Marilyn Boch: "I was working in the Academy's observatory when I saw a gold, oval-shaped flying machine racing through the night sky."

Dr. Marilyn Boch: "Sightings of this nature are quite common but rarely reported."

Dr. Marilyn Boch: "Other scientists have also seen UFOs but have not reported them because they don't want to jeopardize their reputations."

Dr. Marilyn Boch: "The government is putting pressure on the scientific community to withhold information about UFO sightings in order to avoid mass panic."

Grammar Focus 2

Exercise A

The interviewer asked Noel...

1. ...how often he read his horoscope.
2. ...if he had ever had paranormal experiences.
3. ...how many supernatural phenomena he had experienced in his life.
4. ...if he knew what "psychokinesis" was.
5. ...when he had experienced his most recent paranormal experience.
6. ...if he thought he was psychic. / ...if he thinks he is psychic.
7. ...if he would participate in / consider participating in an experiment involving levitation.
8. ...if he would call the office to confirm the time of the experiment.

Exercise B

Possible answers:

1. The boy on the terrace shouted that Daniel was just in time to play ball.
2. Daniel's friends asked him if he was alright.
3. José's mother told him that the people who lived in the house were on vacation and that they had left their keys with José's parents.
4. José's father said that Daniel must have landed on the old chair and that the old chair had broken his fall.
5. At first, Daniel thought it had been a great coincidence. Later, he concluded that his guardian angel had moved that chair from somewhere else to save his life.

Exercise C

Answers will vary.

Grammar Expansion

Exercise D

1. The father shouted to his son to stop the nonsense.
2. "Do not be afraid," the shaman told him.
3. "Be careful!" said the clairvoyant.
4. She ordered her husband to get the camera.
5. The medium warned the listeners to beware of a man with a blond beard.

Exercise E

Answers will vary.

Writing

Exercise A

7, 4, 6, 8, 2, 5, 10, 3, 1, 9 or
7, 5, 4, 8, 2, 3, 10, 6, 1, 9

Exercises B and C

Answers will vary.

Exercise D

What I remember most about my arrival in this country was a feeling of hope. We arrived early one ice-cold winter morning in February. My mother and father were very exhausted, having travelled for so long with four young children. I was ten. When we stepped off the plane and looked around us at the grey, icy terminal buildings, my father said that he <u>was</u> not sure he <u>would be able to / could</u> live here. My mother took his hand and told him not to judge a whole country on its international airport. Still, my father insisted he <u>could</u> feel heaviness in <u>his</u> bones. "We <u>will</u> struggle here," he said. We children were very excited despite our lack of sleep, and sadness at having left behind friends and relations. But on the walk from the plane to the terminal I felt a deep, cold chill creeping through my thin sweater. I began to feel tired, very tired and at that moment I cursed under my breath that perhaps my father <u>was</u> right. Perhaps we had made a mistake. My mother must have guessed my thoughts for she hugged me warmly, and looking into my innocent eyes, soothed me, saying that our arrival <u>was / had been</u> a blessing. With tears in my eyes, I looked up at her face. As I glanced beyond her shoulders, a faint but steady ray of sunshine was creeping through a crack in the thick winter clouds. It felt warm and soothing. I recognized it as an omen, and, as the weak sun bathed my face, I knew that she was right. Our arrival <u>was</u> a blessing. Taking my father's hand, I walked towards the terminal building with a sense of renewed hope.

Exercise E

Answers will vary.

Exercise A

1. a
2. b
3. c
4. a
5. b
6. b
7. a
8. c
9. a
10. b
11. b
12. a
13. a
14. c
15. b
16. a
17. c
18. a
19. a
20. b

Exercise B

1. ap / pro̊ach
2. chål / lenge
3. con / clů / sion
4. di / me̊n / sions
5. e̊ / ner / gy
6. ex / po̊ / sure
7. fi̊ / nal
8. fůnc / tion
9. i̊n / di / cate
10. in / ves / ti / gå / tion
11. in / vo̊lved
12. i̊ / tems
13. jo̊b
14. lå / bour
15. me̊n / tal
16. per / ce̊ived
17. pre / di̊c / ted
18. pro / je̊ct
19. re / li̊ / ance
20. sta / bi̊l / i / ty

Exercise C

1. (adj) approaching, approachable
2. (adj) challenging   (v)challenge
3. (v)conclude   (adj) concluding
4. (adj) energetic / energized   (adv) energetically
5. (v) expose   (adj) exposed
6. (adv) finally
7. (adj) functioning, functional   (adv) functionally
8. (n) indication
9. (v) investigate
10. (n) involvement
11. (v) itemize
12. (n) mentality   (adv) mentally
13. (n) perception
14. (adj) (un)predictable   (adv) predictably
15. (n) projection
16. (n) reliability   (v) rely   (adj) reliable
17. (adj) stable

Exercise D

Answers will vary.

Exercise E

1. energy
2. job
3. involved
4. projects
5. challenge
6. rely
7. labour
8. items
9. finally
10. functioning
11. approached
12. investigate
13. perception
14. indicated
15. concluded
16. exposed
17. dimension
18. mentally
19. stable
20. predicted

Unit 3

Grammar Focus 1

Exercise A

	DETERMINER	SIZE	GENERAL DESCRIPTION	AGE	SHAPE	COLOUR	MATERIAL	ORIGIN	PURPOSE
EXAMPLE	many	medium-sized		ancient			stone		
1	single	small	intricately carved			black	onyx		fertility
2	three	colossal	majestic		pointy	blue-hazed			
3	hundreds	small	pristine			crystal-clear			
4	countless		interesting			rust-coloured		Aboriginal	religious
5	their	large	formerly grand	ancient	dome-shaped				

Exercise B
1. all adventurous
2. moderately long, scenic
3. Narrow, curving, man-made
4. small, natural
5. heavy, waterproof
6. countless, unusual
7. vast, white, sandy
8. large, ten-year-old wood

Exercise C
Possible answers:
1. a jolly round white snowman
2. a miniature manicured Japanese bonsai tree
3. a fierce-looking carved Indonesian ceremonial mask
4. an ancient fierce-looking terracotta warrior
5. majestic snow-capped Swiss alps

Exercise D
1. razor
2. dog food
3. ice cream / milkshake / frozen yogurt
4. dishwashing liquid
5. liquid refreshment (pop, etc.)
6. clothing
7. cookware
8. soap
9. paint
10. doll

Exercises E and F
Answers will vary.

Vocabulary

Exercise A

dangerous: perilous

expert: skilful

magnificent: outstanding

renowned: famous

smooth: undisturbed

traditional: conventional

Exercise B

Noun	Verb	Adjective	Adverb
bravery	brave	brave	bravely
adventure		adventurous	adventurously
dedication	dedicate	dedicated	
courage		courageous	courageously
inspiration	inspire	inspirational / inspire / inspiring	
perseverance	persvere	persevering	

Exercise C

Possible answers:

1. densely populated, well-maintained
2. spectacular piece of expressive architecture
3. delicately spiced
4. hospitable
5. minuscule, yet intricately carved
6. lively, entertaining, and very skillful
7. distinguished-looking
8. smooth and uneventful
9. frigid
10. awe-inspiring

Vocabulary Expansion 1

Exercise D

Possible answers:

1. Switzerland is considerably more expensive than Mexico.
2. Thai food is a bit hotter than Indonesian food.
3. The Japanese bullet train is substantially faster than the express train.
4. First class is much more comfortable than economy airline seats.
5. The temperature in Ecuador is slightly warmer than the temperature in southern Colombia.

Grammar Focus 2

Exercise A

1. that / which
2. which
3. whom / that
4. which
5. which
6. which
7. who / that

Exercise B

Possible answers:

1. Barb, who had never been out of Canada, flew to Thailand.
2. There, she met her sister, who had been living in Japan.
3. They enjoyed the food, which was hot and spicy.
4. They slept in guest houses that were clean, cheap, and comfortable.
5. In the market, she bought a beautiful tapestry at a good price, over which she had haggled.
6. Barb rode an elephant, which could carry two people, while trekking in northern Thailand.
7. The sisters, who had a lot of catching up to do, had a great time.
8. They saw some traditional dancers, who were very skilled and graceful.
9. The temples, which were extremely ornate, were awe-inspiring.
10. It was a great experience which she will probably never have the opportunity to repeat.

Exercise C

Possible answers:

1. ...enjoys travelling to faraway parts of the world.
2. ...have unusual architecture and museums with exhibits of cultural interest.
3. ...look unusual but appetizing.
4. ...don't have enough food to eat.
5. ...I haven't visited is India.
6. ...capture the lives of everyday people.
7. ...few tourists have been before.
8. ...the temperature is consistently over 40 degrees.

Grammar Expansion

Exercise D

The following words should be crossed out:

1. that (direct object)
2. whom (object of preposition)
3. not possible
4. who is (relative clause contains relative pronoun + be)
5. that (indirect object)
6. that (direct object)
7. not possible
8. which (direct object)

Exercise E

(1) (Mount Everest), which is located on the border between Nepal and China, (NR)

(4) (Sir Edmund Hillary), who was a new Zealand mountaineer and explorer, (NR)

(10) (Pasquale Scaturro)—who is the founder and president of Exploration Specialists, an international geophysical and exploration company, (NR)

(13) (1995), when he got all the way to the South Summit, at 8,750 metres (NR)

(18) (ridge), where one wrong step would send climbers plunging either 2,400 metres or 3,050 metres to their deaths, (R)

(23) (woman) who had collapsed in the snow and was in serious distress. (R)

(27) (feat) which probably saved her life (R)

(29) (Everest Environmental Expedition), which was a group of climbers dedicated to preserving the natural environment. (NR)

(34) (debris) that had been left by previous climbers (R)

(39) (oxygen bottles, batteries, trash, and human waste) that had been left on the mountain face by previous adventurers (R)

(42) (attempt) that brought him the most notoriety. (R)

(43) (National Federation of the Blind), which pledged $250,000 to sponsor the climb (NR)

(45) (ascent) that took several months. (R)

(46) (climber) who was the first legally blind person to ever make an attempt. (R)

(49) (Time magazine), which called it one of the most successful Mount Everest expeditions in history (NR)

(52) (records) which included the first blind person to ever scale the mountain (R)

(55) (Weihenmayer), who was the blind climber (NR)

(56) (Bull) who was the oldest man to climb Everest (NR)

Exercise F

Possible answers:

1. Climbers who attempt to ascend Mount Everest must be in good health.
2. The Everest Environmental Expedition, which climbed in 1998, removed garbage from the mountain.
3. Garbage which litters the mountain is a disgrace.
4. The weather, which is extremely harsh, often prevents successful climbs.
5. Sherpas, who are expert mountaineers, guide climbers to the summit.
6. The book that Weihenmayer wrote is called *Touch the Top of the World*.
7. Climbing records that were broken include the oldest climber to summit.
8. Erik Weihenmayer, who is legally blind, climbed Mount Everest.

Vocabulary Expansion 2

Exercise A

1. in danger of losing everything
2. try very hard; try one's best
3. have no specific plan in mind; do things as they come
4. about to quit; totally exhausted
5. to fail
6. what interests some may not interest others

Exercise B

1. play it by ear
2. different strokes for different folks
3. gave it his best shot
4. on its last legs
5. on the line
6. blow it

Writing

Exercise A

The following sentences should be eliminated:

- Australia is a former British penal colony.
- Sydney is located in the state of New South Wales.
- Opera music can be truly inspirational, although some say it is an acquired taste.

Exercise B

Answers will vary.

Exercise C

Answers will vary.

Exercises D and E

Answers will vary.

Academic Word List

Exercise A

1. g
2. j
3. a
4. e
5. h
6. i
7. b
8. c
9. f
10. d
11. p
12. q
13. k
14. t

15. m
16. l
17. s
18. n
19. r
20. o

Exercise B

1. **bĕn** / e / fit
2. **cĭv** / il
3. **cŏm** / pon / ents
4. con / **sĭs** / tent
5. **cŭl** / tur / al
6. dis / **tĭnc** / tion
7. **dŏm** / i / nant
8. en / **sŭre**
9. e / **quă** / tion
10. e / **quĭv** / a / lent
11. fa / **cĭl** / i / tate
12. im / **pŏsed**
13. in / ter / **ăc** / tion
14. per / **spĕc** / tive
15. **sĕc** / tion
16. se / **cŭ** / ri / ty
17. **sĭm** / i / lar
18. **sĭte**
19. **sŏurce**
20. tech / **nĭques**

Exercise C

1. (adj) beneficial
2. (n) civilian / civilization   (adv) civilly
3. (n) consistency   (adv) consistently
4. (adj) cultured
5. (adj) distinctive / indistinct   (adv) distinctively / distinctly
6. (n) dominance / domination   (adv) dominantly
7. (v) equate
8. (n) equivalence
9. (n) facilitation / facility
10. (n) imposition   (adj) imposing
11. (n) interaction   (adv) interactively
12. (adj) perspective
13. (v) secure
14. (n) similarity   (adv) similarly
15. (adj) technical   (adv) technically

Exercise D

Answers will vary.

Exercise E

1. civilization
2. cultures
3. interaction
4. ensures
5. perspectives
6. beneficial
7. distinct
8. source
9. consistently
10. impose
11. techniques
12. similar
13. components
14. dominant
15. facilitator
16. site
17. secure
18. section
19. equivalent
20. equate

Unit 4

Vocabulary 1

Exercise A

a) to understand, to comprehend, to grasp the main idea of something, to perceive the main argument
b) to not understand, to not get the main idea
c) to get off topic, to get distracted from main discussion point, to talk about something unrelated, to move discussion away from the main topic
d) to avoid saying something directly, to talk around the main issue without stating it directly
e) to discover through gossip, to hear a rumour
f) to force a comment, to make someone tell something, to get someone to be precise

Vocabulary Expansion

Exercise B1

a) Let off steam: to say something in a way that helps you to get rid of frustrations
b) Shoot the breeze: have an informal conversation
c) Be on the same page: have the same perspective
d) Cut off: interrupt
e) Get to the point: say exactly what you mean in a direct way
f) Biting your tongue: keeping quiet
g) Turn you off: annoys you so that you lose interest
h) Tune out: stop paying attention
i) Tuned in: paying attention
j) Checking in: communicating with someone regularly to clarifying that something has been understood or to see how things are going

Exercise B2

a) bit my tongue
b) tunes out
c) cut off
d) let off steam
e) turns me off
f) shoot the breeze
g) listen up
h) were on the same page
i) let off steam
j) get to the point

Grammar Focus 1

Exercise A

Possible answers:

1. even though / although
2. but / yet
3. despite

4. in spite of the fact that / although / even though
5. whereas / while / even though
6. whereas / while
7. although / even though / yet / in spite of the fact that

Exercise B

Answers will vary.

Vocabulary 2

Exercise A

	Incorrect	Correct
1.	challenging	concise
2.	photocopying	interpersonal
3.	supervisor	barrier
4.	computers	cues
5.	lazy	vague
6.	paper	feedback
7.	wrote	gestured
8.	inappropriate	perceptive
9.	unfortunate	interactive
10.	briefcase	message

Grammar Focus 2

Exercise A

Note: Sentence structure will vary depending on the expressions used.

1. even so / still / nevertheless / nonetheless / however
2. on the contrary
3. however / nevertheless / nonetheless / still
4. on the other hand / however
5. still / nonetheless / nevertheless
6. however / still / even so
7. however / still / even so / nonetheless / nevertheless

Grammar Expansion

Exercise B

1. (19) to establish a general feeling or atmosphere
2. (25) to do something without fail or with great commitment
3. (42) get off to a bad start
4. (43) to have a good relationship with someone
5. (48) to not be kept informed about things
6. (64) person who works with figures (accountant)
7. (71) availability for people at all times
8. (75) to take care of someone/to guide someone's actions so closely that you are almost doing the action yourself
9. (86) to gossip about someone

Exercise C

1. but: lines 11, 16, 100
   yet: 95

2. although: 30, 71
while: 64, 77, 91
whereas: 11
in spite of the fact that: 100

3. however: 66
on the contrary: 103
even so: 48
on the other hand: 84
still: 43 (Not used here with the meaning "despite that", but rather with the meaning of "continuing.")

Exercise D

Possible answers:

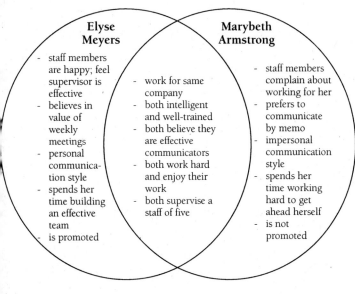

Elyse Meyers
- staff members are happy; feel supervisor is effective
- believes in value of weekly meetings
- personal communication style
- spends her time building an effective team
- is promoted

(overlap)
- work for same company
- both intelligent and well-trained
- both believe they are effective communicators
- both work hard and enjoy their work
- both supervise a staff of five

Marybeth Armstrong
- staff members complain about working for her
- prefers to communicate by memo
- impersonal communication style
- spends her time working hard to get ahead herself
- is not promoted

Exercise E

Note: Sentence structure will vary depending on the expressions of contrast used.

1. Incorrect: whereas / while / on the other hand / however
2. Incorrect: but / however / still / nevertheless
3. Incorrect: whereas / while / on the other hand
4. Incorrect: in spite of the fact that / even though / although / nevertheless
5. Correct
6. Correct
7. Incorrect: while / whereas / yet / on the other hand
8. Correct
9. Correct
10. Incorrect: on the other hand / however

Exercise F

Possible answers:

Note: Sentence structure will vary depending on the expressions of contrast used.

1. a) A bilingual child may speak English at school, **yet** switch to Polish, Spanish, or Cantonese at home.
   b) **Although** a bilingual child may speak English at school, he or she may switch to Polish, Spanish, or Cantonese at home.
   c) A bilingual child may speak English at school, **whereas** he or she may switch to Polish, Spanish, or Cantonese at home.

2. a) In one study on...learned English well **while** students who were taught different subjects....
   b) In one study on...learned English well. Students who were taught different...did not learn English well, **however**.
   c) In one study on...learned English well. **On the other hand**, students who were taught different subjects....

3. a) **Even though** it is more difficult to learn a second language in adulthood, it is not impossible.
   b) **Though** it is more difficult to learn a second language in adulthood, it is not impossible.
   c) It is more difficult to learn a second language in adulthood. **Nonetheless**, it is not impossible.

4. a) Sari Kristiina moved to North America in her forties without having learned any English. **Even so**, she managed to learn English with native-like fluency.
   b) **In spite of the fact that** Sari Kristiina moved to North America in her forties without having learned any English, she managed to learn English with native-like fluency.
   c) Sari Kristiina moved to North America in her forties without having learned any English. **Still**, she managed to learn English with native-like fluency.

Writing

Exercise A

Point-by-point method

Exercises B and C

Answers will vary.

Academic Word List

Exercise A

1. properly
2. compares differences
3. fixed
4. loudness
5. power positions
6. idea

7. indicate
8. are like
9. order
10. relationship
11. responded
12. basically
13. kinds of information
14. permission
15. cultural
16. example
17. before
18. understandings or explanations
19. proper
20. actions

Exercise B

1. ap / **prŏp** / ri / ate
2. con / **sĕnt**
3. con / **trăst**
4. **ĕth** / nic
5. fun / da / **mĕn** / tal
6. im / **plĭes**
7. **ĭn** / stance
8. in / ter / pre / **tă** / tion
9. **nŏ** / tion
10. **păr** / al / lel
11. **părt** / ner / ship
12. **prĕ** / vi / ous
13. re / **ăc** / tion
14. re / so / **lŭ** / tion
15. re / **sŏur** / ces
16. **sĕ** / quence
17. **stă** / tus
18. **tăsk**
19. va / **lĭ** / di / ty
20. **vŏl** / ume

Exercise C

1. (adv) appropriately
2. (v) consent   (adj) consenting
3. (n) contrast   (adj) contrasting; contrastive
4. (n) ethnicity
5. (adj) fundamentally
6. (n) implication   (adj) implied
7. (adj) instantaneous   (adv) instantaneously
8. (v) interpret   (adj) interpretive / interpreted
9. (v) parallel   (n) parallelism
10. (v) partner   (adj) partnering
11. (adv) previously
12. (v) react   (adj) reactive / reacting
13. (v) resolve   (adj) resolved
14. (adj) resourceful
15. (v) sequence   (adj) sequential   (adv) sequentially
16. (v) validate   (adj) valid
17. (adj) voluminous

Exercise D

Answers will vary.

Exercise E

1. interpretation
2. appropriate
3. fundamental
4. contrasted
5. ethnic
6. status
7. partnerships
8. task
9. sequence
10. react
11. appropriately
12. resolve
13. instance
14. notion
15. valid
16. resources

Unit 5

Grammar Focus 1

Exercise A

Possible answers:

1. I learned that the technologies portrayed in science fiction often become real technology in the future.
2. I have learned that filmmakers hire scientists to ensure the validity and believability of the science portrayed.
3. I have realized that science fiction gives scientists ideas for new developments.
4. I learned that the technologies of the future are believable because their foundations can be found in existing science and that technologies like brain implants really will be possible in the not too distant future.
5. I now believe that the technologies portrayed in these futuristic shows will actually exist in my lifetime.
6. I feel that Hollywood gives us all a language to talk about future developments and inspires us to make the imaginative real.

Exercise B

Possible answers:

1. …the police used to fly in *Minority Report*…
2. …the backpack provided enough thrust for only 20 seconds…
3. …the military is experimenting with a strap-on helicopter.
4. …a parachute brings them back to earth.

Exercise C

1. Lee is unaware of where the filming will take place.
2. You will be impressed by how many returning stars we have signed.
3. Do you know why she watches the show?
4. Are you aware of when the publicity campaign will kick off?
5. I can't identify who the best actor on the show is.

Exercise D

Possible answers:

1. …I would want to watch the same show several times.
2. …I find the shows appealing.
3. …the attraction was.
4. …the shows had been on the air.
5. …the show had first started.
6. …people would react to his show.
7. …much money he would make.
8. …the appeal of a show like *Star Trek* really is.

Grammar Expansion

Exercise E

Possible answers:

1. I guess so. I have always had an active imagination so science fiction appeals to me.
2. I don't believe so. There has to be some element of the possible to make it appealing.
3. It seems so. The most successful shows do consult scientists regularly.
4. I'm afraid not. Some of them are really bad and not worth watching.
5. I assume so. There will always be people who enjoy the futuristic nature of sci-fi shows.
6. I don't think so. It would really depend on what was being portrayed; maybe if it wasn't too scary or violent.

Exercise F

Noun clauses:

1. that science is tentative, that it is not certain, that it is subject to change
2. that computers will begin to think like men / that men will begin to think like computers
3. that technological advances would benefit mankind

Vocabulary 1

Exercise A

Careful and Systematic Study	Thinking and Reasoning
analysis examination experiment investigation observation research	argument debate example

Exercise B

1. of 2. for / against 3. about / on 4. of
5. of 6. of / with 7. into 8. of 9. into / on / about

Vocabulary Expansion

Exercise D

Idiom	Meaning
be under pressure	suffering from stress
burn the midnight oil	stay up very late to work
roll up one's sleeves and dig in	work hard
figure out	understand, determine
find out	discover
out of the blue	unexpectedly
in the nick of time	at the last moment

Grammar Focus 2

Exercise A

1. that governments have strict regulations about how far scientists can go with experiments.
   (*it* + *be* + a + noun + noun clause)
2. That aliens have visited earth (subject)
3. that we can grow human organs (after a noun)
4. that we will be making regular trips to other planets in the near future. (complement of *be*)
5. that scientists will try to grow a human heart in the future. (*it* + *seems* + adjective + noun clause)
6. who was responsible for the mix-up. (after a preposition)
7. that his view of the future would be shared by others. (after an adjective of feeling or opinion)

Exercise B

Possible answers:

1. That computers are taking over some people's jobs worries me.
2. Whether stem cell research is ethical or not is of concern to everyone.
3. That scientists have already been able to grow some organs supports the notion that soon researchers will be able to grow other human organs.
4. That governments have banned studies using cells from embryos demonstrates that many people are uncomfortable with stem cell research.
5. That jobs are being lost due to technological change is a huge problem.
6. That scientists should use stem cells in their research is not universally accepted.

Exercise C

Possible answers:

1. The fact that police must now monitor the Internet is pathetic.
2. The idea that a computer could be portable was inconceivable 40 years ago.
3. The discovery that hydrogen and oxygen can be combined to make a clean fuel for our future is fantastic.

4. The news that malfunctioning genes may be repaired in the future has given hope to many individuals.
5. The idea that you can take an exotic vacation without leaving home appeals to some people.

Exercise D

Possible answers:

1. I am especially interested in what the mission to Mars will reveal about the possibilities of life on that planet.
2. Do you honestly approve of what scientists are doing with genetic manipulation?
3. The studies focus on whether or not life is possible on Mars.
4. In the future, scientists will look at the possibility that cities could be built on Mars.
5. People cannot rely on what they hear or read in media reports about UFOs.
6. Do you agree with who they want to send on the first mission to Mars?

Exercise E

1. People asked why the scientists wanted to do this type of experiment.
2. The scientists indicated to them that they hoped to use stem cells to reverse diseases. *Or* The scientists indicated that they hoped to use stem cells to reverse diseases
3. The people asked the scientists if they had considered the possible negative implications.
4. According to the scientists, it was important that this type of research be done despite the possible negative implications.
5. The people told the scientists that they would like to see experiments with stem cells taken from human embryos stopped immediately
6. What that would do is prevent scientists from creating human clones.
7. Working together, the people and scientists discussed how they could continue research in a way that does not involve stem cells taken from embryos.

Vocabulary 2

Exercise A

Possible answers:

astrochemistry / astrograph / astrological / astrologist / astrology / astronaut / astronomy / astrophysics

biochemistry / biodegradable / biological / biologist / biology / biophysics / biopsy / biorhythm

cyclometer / cyclone

dynamic / dynamism / dynamo / dynasty

geocentric / geological / geologist / geology / geometry / geopolitics / geophysics

lithograph / paragraph / photograph / telegraph / autograph

pathogen / pathological / pathologist / pathology

Exercise B

Answers will vary.

Writing

Exercise A

Possible answers:

Outline 1: Automation has resulted in the need for fewer workers.

Outline 2: Many women do what they can to help in the fight against AIDS.

Exercise B

Controlling ideas:

1. enabled us to explore areas where no human has visited
2. gone too far
3. successful spin-offs

Exercise C

1. Hollywood has produced several science-fiction movies, now considered classics, that have given us possible glimpses of our future.
2. possible glimpses of our future.
3. Examples are sequenced from past to most recent.
4. a. a future where humans are divided into two distinct groups—thinkers and workers
   b. flight to Jupiter and a world where computers may be superior to man
   c. travel to other galaxies and interactions with their inhabitants
   d. a fake world that the machine-made android-like humans have created to control humans

Exercise D

Outline 1

Topic Sentence: Downsizing in companies as a result of technological advances has had a tremendous personal impact on workers.

Example 1: It is a fact that many men in their late fifties who have been laid off have been unable to rejoin the workforce, and consequently lose everything they ever had.

Example 2: It's the idea that they are no longer useful that leads some men into personal depression.

Example 3: It's been documented that men who lose their jobs sometimes have serious problems with their families.

Outline 2

Topic Sentence: Advances in technology have created increasingly destructive weapons of war.

Example 1: That soldiers could only kill when at arm's length from each other had limited casualties to some extent.

Example 2: The fact that guns enabled soldiers to kill at great distances increased the bloodshed in conflicts incredibly.

Example 3: The fact that nuclear bombs can instantly annihilate everything within a wide radius of landing has brought unlimited killing capacity to war.

Exercises E and F

Answers will vary.

Academic Word List

Exercise A

1. construction
2. contribution
3. link
4. normal
5. create
6. credit
7. role
8. constraint
9. transfer
10. economic
11. evolution
12. computer
13. phase
14. medical
15. philosophy
16. evidence
17. concept
18 despite
19. grant
20. minorities

Exercise B

1. com / **pǔt** / er
2. **cǒn** / cept
3. con / **straïnts**
4. con / **strǔc** / tion
5. con / tri / **bǔ** / tion
6. cre / **åte**
7. **crě** / dit
8. de / **spite**
9. ec /o / **nǒm** / ic
10. **ěv** / i / dence
11. ev / o / **lǔ** / tion
12. **grånt** / ed
13. **lǐnk**
14. **mě** / di /cal
15. mi / **nǒr** / i / ties
16. **nǒr** / mal
17. **phåse**
18. phi / **lǒs** / o / phy
19. **rǒle**
20. **trǎns** / fer

Exercise C

1. (v) compute   (adj) computerized / computational
2. (v) conceive   (adj) conceptual   (adv) conceptually
3. (v) constrain   (adj) constrained / unconstrained
4. (v) construct   (adj) constructive
5. (v) contribute
6. (n) creation / creativity / creator   (adj) creative
   (adv) creatively
7. (n) creditor / credit
8. (n) economy / economist   (adv) economically
9. (adj) evidential
10. (v) evolve
11. (n) grant
12. (adj) linked
13. (adj) minor
14. (n) medicine
15. (adv) normally
16. (v) philosophize   (adj) philosophical
    (adv) philosophically
17. (adj) transferable

Exercise D

Answers will vary.

Exercise E

1. role
2. normal
3. grants
4. created
5. reconstruct
6. despite
7. constraints
8. evidence
9. contributions
10. economic
11. medical
12. minor
13. credited
14. computers
15. concept
16. evolved
17. phase
18. link
19. transfer
20. philosophy

Unit 6

Vocabulary 1

Exercise A

(2)   reason
(4)   conclusions
(5)   analogies
(14)   logical
(40)   wisdom
(41)   arguments
(43)   biased

Exercise B

1. analogous
2. knowledgeable
3. opinion
4. wisdom
5. bias
6. spatial
7. argument
8. puzzled

Grammar Focus 1

Exercise A

1. g
2. e
3. d
4. a
5. h
6. b
7. f
8. c

Exercise B

1. Incorrect ...if I had thought more critically.
2. Correct
3. Incorrect ...his intellect would develop more / If the parents had provided a more stimulating environment...
4. Incorrect ...if they read a variety of materials
5. Correct
6. Incorrect ...you would be much smarter.
7. Correct

Exercise C

1. If Randa didn't value education, she wouldn't study so hard.
2. If Peter had not been interested in science as a young man, he wouldn't (might not) have become an engineer.
3. If Margaret weren't a teacher, she wouldn't know what will be expected of her children when they get to high school.
4. If Cosmo had liked to write, he would have written more often.

5. If Tina didn't take her young daughter Chloë to the library every week, Chloë wouldn't feel so comfortable there.
6. If Chris hadn't begun piano lessons at the age of four, now—at the age of six—he wouldn't play so well.
7. If Nicholas weren't so interested in science, his mother would not have sent him to science camp in the summer.
8. If young Martin didn't spend so much time with his Spanish-speaking grandparents, he wouldn't speak Spanish as well as English.

Exercise D

Answers will vary.

Vocabulary 2

Exercise A

1. focus on
2. figure out
3. find out
4. working towards
5. accounted for
6. bring about

Exercise B

1. to focus: to adjust a lens in order to see clearly; to make clear
            to direct something onto a point

   to focus on: to concentrate on
               to direct attention to

2. to figure: to believe, think, conclude

   to figure out: to discover
                to think about until you understand

3. to account: to think or consider (She accounted him a good writer.)

   to account for: to explain

4. to work: to have a job
           to make an effort to do something
           to function, operate, control

   to work towards: to try to reach or achieve a goal

5. to bring: to cause to come
            to carry to

   to bring about: to make something happen

6. to find: to look for and get back after a search
          to get or discover after a search

   to find out: to learn by study or inquiry
              to discover

Exercise C

Answers will vary.

Grammar Focus 2

Exercise A

a. The victim must have screamed.

b. The cook could have killed him.

c. The maid might have seen the murderer.

d. The wife probably didn't kill him.

e. The president couldn't have committed suicide. / The president didn't commit suicide.

Grammar Expansion

Exercise B

Possible answers:

1. If you want to do well on the test, you will have to study hard.
2. If you know one foreign language, it should be easier to learn another.
3. If you don't read the book, you will not be able to write the summary.
4. If the suspect has an alibi, he can't have committed the murder. / If the suspect can't supply an alibi, he might have committed the murder.
5. If you knew something about Middle Eastern history, you might understand the context of the president's speech better.

Exercise C

1. If you are trying to solve a problem, your first step should be to interpret or represent the problem correctly.
2. The "tactic of elimination" strategy will only work if your list of possible solutions contains at least one good solution to the problem.
3. If the "tactic of elimination" strategy is not suitable for solving a problem, you can try visualizing or creative problem-solving.
4. If you cannot find a solution to a problem after careful, step-by-step efforts, you should stop thinking about the problem for a while and return to it later, approaching it from a new angle.
5. If you reject a prospective solution at first glance, you may be rejecting a solution that may solve your problem.

Exercise D

Note: Some variations may exist according to interpretation of context.

1. If all carnivores eat meat, and my pet is a carnivore, then my pet must eat meat.
2. If polar bears are white, and this bear lives at the North Pole, then this bear must be white.
3. If Henry lost his dog that answers to the name of Fado, and Jeannie found a dog that answers to the name of Fado, then the dog Jeannie found might be the dog Henry lost.

4. If Martin's grandparents speak only Spanish, and Martin spends a lot of time with them, then he probably speaks (might speak) Spanish, too.
5. If you have no brothers, then Pat must be your sister / then Pat must be a woman's name.
6. If Paula does not read science-fiction novels, then the novel she is reading now cannot be a science fiction novel.
7. If the teacher received an essay from an unidentified student about the ethics of genetic engineering, only two students wrote an essay on this topic, and John wrote an essay on illegal organ transplants, then John did not write the essay on the ethics of genetic engineering.
8. If Anita's mother is Francophone, and Anita has lived in English-speaking Edmonton all her life, but Anita speaks English and French, she might have learned French from her mother.

Exercise E

Answers will vary.

Vocabulary Expansion

Exercise A

Cause: (5, 22) source of, (17) imposed (by), (13) result from, (24, 25) because (of)

Effect: (11) lead to, (13) result in, (14) forced to

Additional expressions

Cause: caused by, reasons for

Effect: consequence of

Exercise B

Answers will vary.

Writing

Exercises A and B

Answers will vary.

Exercise C

If I teach my children only one skill, it <u>will</u> be to learn how to learn. In our rapidly changing technological society, if one can't learn new skills quickly and adapt to new ideas, one <u>is</u> lost. Gone are the days when rote learning led the way to knowledge and success. As little as 50 years ago, if you <u>were</u> knowledgeable, you <u>were</u> admired. If you had a college or university degree, you were guaranteed a good job. If knowledge is all you can offer an employer today, you're not worth hiring; today's knowledge will be obsolete tomorrow. However, if you <u>know</u> where and how to access knowledge, you have a transferable skill that will never become obsolete. If you can <u>understand</u> how you, as an individual, learn best, and can acquire the skills for learning, your road <u>will be</u> paved with opportunity. If, on the other hand, you focus only on what you are learning, without ever understanding the process, each new learning experience <u>may (will) lead</u> to frustration and possibly failure.

Exercise D

Answers will vary.

Academic Word List

Exercise A

1. b
2. a
3. c.
4. a
5. b
6. a
7. c
8. a
9. b
10. a
11. c
12. b
13. a
14. b
15. c
16. b
17. a
18. a
19. c
20. a

Exercise B

1. ad / **jŭst** / ment
2. ap / **prŏx** / i / ma / ted
3. as / **sŭme**
4. au / **thŏr** / i / ty
5. **cŏn** / text
6. de / **dŭc** / tion
7. **gŏals**
8. im / mi / **grå** / tion
9. **lĕ** / gal
10. **lŏ** / gic
11. **mȧin** / ten / ance
12. pro / **mŏte**
13. **pŭb** / lished
14. **rĕl** / e / vant
15. res / **pŏnse**
16. spe / **cĭ** / fic
17. sta / **tĭs** / tics
18. **strȧt** / e / gies
19. suf / **fĭ** / cient
20. **sŭr** / vey

Exercise C

1. (v) adjust (adj) adjusted
2. (n) approximation (adj) approximate
   (adv) approximately
3. (n) assumption (n) (adj) assumed / assuming
4. (v) authorize (adj) authoritative (adv) authoritatively
5. (v) contextualize (adj) contextualized / contextual
6. (v) to deduce (adj) deductive
7. (v) immigrate
8. (v) legalize (n) legality
9. (adj) logical (adv) logically
10. (v) maintain
11. (n) promotion
12. (v) publish
13. (n) relevance
14. (v) respond (adj) responsive
15. (v) specify (n) specification
16. (adj) statistical
17. (v) strategize (adj) strategic (adv) strategically
18. (v) suffice (adv) sufficiently
19. (v) survey (adj) surveyed

Exercise D

Answers will vary.

Exercise E

1. promoted
2. authority
3. published
4. sufficient
5. relevant
6. logical
7. statistical
8. specific
9. responses
10. context
11. adjust
12. immigration
13. surveys
14. approximately
15. legal
16. goal
17. maintain
18. assumption
19. strategy
20. deduce

Unit 7

Vocabulary 1

Exercise A

1. appeal
2. hyped
3. trivia
4. idols
5. mania
6. trends
7. logo

r	t	i	l	f	k	a	p	k	l	m
t	r	r	d	o	s	l	o	d	i	l
g	i	m	m	i	g	k	s	e	b	h
n	v	o	a	t	o	c	p	t	c	
h	i	p	n	i	n	r	i	y	c	g
m	a	n	i	a	e	a	k	h	d	i
e	l	a	p	p	e	a	l	l	a	m
r	n	o	e	r	t	r	e	n	d	s

Exercise B

1. idolize
2. trivial
3. crazy
4. appealing
5. trendy
6. manic
7. hyped

Exercise C

Answers will vary.

Grammar Focus

Exercise A

Possible answers:

1. even though / although
2. since
3. even if
4. once
5. as long as / once
6. while / even though / although
7. as if
8. unless
9. whereas
10. while / although

Exercise B

Possible answers:

1. <u>Once</u> she learned how to play the guitar, she picked up the violin and viola easily.
2. The actor stopped his monologue in the middle of the sentence <u>as though</u> he had forgotten his lines.
3. His parents persuaded him to study music at college <u>since</u> they knew that it would be difficult to make a good living being a musician.
4. We can visit the art museum tomorrow <u>provided that</u> it is open on Sundays.
5. She got the lead role in the film <u>in spite of the fact</u> that she was not a professional actress.
6. Leslie set her television to record her favourite soap opera at 3:30 p.m. <u>in case</u> she was not home from school on time to watch it.
7. The parents only watched television at night <u>after</u> their young children had gone to bed.
8. The dancer danced <u>as though</u> he were a professional dancer.

Exercise C

Possible answers:

1. Contrast: despite the fact / in spite of the fact that / even though / although / while
2. Condition: as long as / while / provided that / if
3. Reason: because / since
4. Manner: as if / as though
5. Contrast: even though / although / in spite of the fact that
6. Condition: unless / until
7. Time: since
8. Time: once / when / as soon as

Exercise D

1. c
2. f
3. h
4. a
5. j
6. i
7. e
8. g
9. d
10. b

Exercise E

Possible answers:

1. North America has had a notoriously poor independent music scene because there are not enough local venues that support independent musicians
2. Canada's independent music scene will not improve unless local venues begin to support local musicians.
3. It was difficult for independent artists to distribute their music before networking sites like MySpace were available.
4. Apple's iTunes is successful even though people first scoffed at the idea of paying for music online.

5. Once networking sites like MySpace became available anyone with a microphone and Internet connection could record their music for the public.
6. Now than independent music is more accessible, people are beginning to take notice.

Exercise F
Answers will vary.

Vocabulary 2

Exercise A

Clue	Idiom
Too much humiliation is unacceptable.	get out of hand
If you cannot watch scenes with blood and bruising…	the faint of heart
While it's not nice to laugh at other people's misfortunes…	poke fun at
That must be difficult to manage.	deal with
I just couldn't learn them.	get the hang of
I don't invite them onto my friends list…	shut out
…meet with friends face-to-face.	hang out with
…they don't have to depend on…	take charge of
…has revealed…	come to light
…difficult to identify a clear, single cause… / confusing	muddy the waters

Exercise B
Answers will vary.

Writing

Exercise A
Title
Girls and Gaming

INTRODUCTION
Thesis Statement: Girls are not as attracted to gaming because of the negative representation of women, the violent themes, and competitive content and design of the games.

BODY
Developmental Paragraph 1
Topic Sentence: One reason girls lose interest in computer games is that in most games, girls do not see themselves represented in positive ways.
Support:
- not many female characters
- female characters are bystanders, not active participants
- large-breasted, thin, scantily dressed
- female characters have role of "damsel in distress," victim, or prize

Developmental Paragraph 2
Topic Sentence: Another reason girls spend less and less time playing computer games as they get older is that the violence in many computer games does not appeal to girls over the long term.
Support:
- Violence makes girls feel bad about themselves
- Research study: more time spent playing violent games decreases self worth, educational achievement, social acceptance

Developmental Paragraph 3
Topic Sentence: A third reason girls lose interest and spend less time gaming as they get older is that the content and design of computer games appeals more to boys than to girls.
Support:
- Girls interested in storylines and exploring characters' personalities, not action and competition
- Girls interested in real-life locations, not fantasy worlds
- Girls interested in communal play, not solo play
- Girls interested in visual design
- Girls interested in communication and relationship aspects of gaming, not winning

CONCLUSION
Topic Sentence: The gender gap in computer gaming can be explained by the fact that computer games are designed by male designers for male audiences.
Concluding Ideas:
- We must encourage girls to become equal participants in scientific and technological evolution.
- The challenge is to design electronic games which appeal not only to boys but also to girls and which build confidence while simultaneously engaging both sexes in sound mathematics and science activity.

Exercises B through E
Answers will vary.

Academic Word List

Exercise A
Part A

1. j		6. e	
2. g		7. f	
3. b		8. c	
4. i		9. a	
5. h		10. d	

Part B

11. o		16. k	
12. m		17. p	
13. s		18. n	
14. r		19. q	
15. t		20. l	

Exercise B

1. **ảc** / cess
2. al / **tểr** / na / tive
3. **cỏm** / ments
4. com / mun / i / **cả** / tion
5. con / **sỉd** / er / a / ble
6. con / sti / **tủ** / tion / al
7. con / **vẻn** / tion
8. dis / tri / **bủ** / tion
9. **ẻm** / pha / sis
10. **ẻx** / port
11. **fẻa** / tures
12. **ỉl** / lus / tra / ted
13. in / di / **vỉ** / du / al
14. in / **vẻst** / ment
15. **nẻt** / work
16. oc / **củr**
17. **phỷ** / si / cal
18. **prỉ** / ma / ry
19. **sỏught**
20. **spẻ** / cif / ied

Exercise C

1. (n) access   (adj) accessible
2. (v) alternate   (adj) alternative
3. (v) comment
4. (v) communicate   (adj) communicative
5. (adv) considerably
6. (n) constitution
7. (v) convene   (adj) conventional
8. (v) distribute
9. (v) emphasize
10. (v) export   (adj) exported / exporting
11. (v) feature   (adj) featuring / featured
12. (n) illustration   (adj) illustrative / illustrated
13. (v) individualize   (adj) individual   (adv) individually
14. (v) invest   (adj) invested
15. (v) network   (adj) networked / networking
16. (n) occurrence
17. (adv) physically
18. (adv) primarily
19. (n) specification   (adj) specific   (adv) specifically

Exercise D

Answers will vary.

Exercise E

1. exports
2. features
3. alternative
4. investment
5. primarily
6. communication
7. networks
8. access
9. distribution
10. conventions
11. illustrated
12. individual
13. sought
14. commentary
15. considerable
16. constitutional
17. specified
18. occurs

Unit 8

Vocabulary

Exercise A

1. i
2. d
3. h
4. e
5. a
6. j
7. f
8. b
9. g
10. c

Exercise B

1. bounce a few ideas (off)
2. to tackle
3. playing hardball
4. clear sailing
5. going downhill
6. ballpark figure
7. wrestle with the hard facts
8. go the distance

Vocabulary Expansion 1

Exercise C

1. badminton racquets
2. baseball gloves
3. soccer balls
4. baseball bats
5. soccer shoes
6. badminton birdies

The three sports are baseball, badminton, and soccer.

Exercise D

Answers will vary.

Grammar Focus 1

Exercise A

Possible answers:

1. I really regret not going to the game last night.
2. He has always avoided stating his opinion that hockey is a violent sport.
3. We discussed organizing a tournament for charity.
4. As a teenager, I disliked not being able to excel in sports.
5. Did they mention buying new equipment at the meeting?
6. Soccer players have to practise dribbling the ball up and down the field.
7. I can't imagine not participating in some kind of physical activity to keep fit.
8. Star athletes can't risk playing with an injury that may end their careers.

Exercise B

Possible answers:

1. I imagine playing soccer isn't that expensive.
2. People keep watching whether it is a real sport or not. I guess it depends on your definition of a real sport.
3. I can't help thinking that playing co-ed sports helps develop respect.
4. I understand participating in both kinds of sports is challenging.
5. I suggest trying synchronized swimming before making such a statement.

Exercise C

1. The figure skater increased his speed by sharpening his skates.
2. Tony won the Olympic 100-metre dash by running the fastest race of his life.
3. Ken accommodated the changing snow conditions by changing the wax on his skis.
4. Michael ensured his racquet was in top shape by restringing it.
5. The baseball player ended the game by catching a fly ball.
6. Chandra won the tournament by bowling a perfect game.

Exercise D

1. Ken is concerned about being able to afford his son's hockey equipment.
2. I'm very excited about going to Wimbledon to watch the tennis finals.
3. He is very good at scoring goals.
4. Marnie McBean and Kathleen Heddle are really proud of having the most Olympic medals for rowing won by any Canadian.
5. The new arena is very suitable playing hockey.
6. They are tired of always arguing when they play tennis.
7. The team is worried about winning the next game. *Or* The team is worried about making the playoffs.
8. He's afraid of diving from the high board.

Exercise E

1. on going
2. of sitting / of staying
3. to losing
4. at sticking
5. of failing

Exercise F

1. We can't have him draining the wading pool early.
2. I resent his (the referee) constantly making calls in favour of the other team.
3. Everyone appreciates her (Jolene) playing at the top of her game.
4. I don't mind them (the neighbourhood children) playing road hockey on our street.
5. They appreciate her (Shari) giving them swimming lessons.

Exercise G

1. hoping / planning — complement of verb
2. diving / swimming — object position after certain verb

3. diving / swimming   - subject
4. rewarding / exciting - complement of verb
5. returning   - object of preposition

Exercise H

Possible answers:

1. ...playing someone not as skilled as she is.
2. ...playing demanding sports like tennis.
3. ...socializing while playing a sport.
4. ...developing physical fitness and endurance.
5. ...taking part in strenuous sports.
6. ...participating in sports that don't give a physical workout.
7. ...having a close match.
8. ...playing a leisurely game.
9. ...improving their hand-eye coordination.
10. ...meeting potential clients on the course.

Exercise I

Answers will vary.

Vocabulary Expansion 2

Exercise A

1. i
2. f
3. h
4. c
5. l
6. k
7. j
8. e
9. g
10. a
11. b
12. d

Exercise B

Possible answers:

Swimming: stroke, float, splash, kick, dive
Soccer: boot, head, kick, pass, guard, dribble
Tennis: slam, run, smash, return, serve
Mountain Biking: spin, balance, ride, jump, pedal
Basketball: dribble, slam, dunk, pass, throw
Skiing: jump, glide, freestyle, lift, balance, tilt, turn

Exercise C

Answers will vary.

Exercise D

Degree of Intensity	Intensifiers
A small degree	a bit, slightly, kind of, a little, a touch of, sort of
A moderate degree	reasonably, rather, somewhat, pretty, quite
A large degree	very, really, substantially, much, awfully, considerably, extremely

Exercise E

Possible answers:

1. a bit
2. extremely
3. somewhat
4. a little
5. really
6. reasonably

Grammar Focus 2

Exercise A

1. The object of ultimate Frisbee is to get the most goals.
2. They try to catch the disc in the opposing team's end zone in order to score a goal.
3. Teammates should try to get into an open space away from the other team to catch the disc.
4. Lugers lie flat on the luge board to decrease wind resistance and increase their speed.
5. They are required to wear helmets and race suits to protect their bodies.
6. Lugers wear sturdy shoes to use as brakes and for controlling the speed.

Exercise B

Answers will vary, but the infinitive form is required after each sentence's starter.

Exercise C

1. to participate / to take part
2. to consider
3. to stand
4. to follow
5. to hire
6. to qualify
7. to perform
8. to take part/to participate

Possible answers:

a) Olympic athletes are expected to practise before a tournament or they will not make the top three.
b) It is very expensive to hire good coaches.
c) Taking part in the Olympics is a thrill of a lifetime.
d) It is important to practise, practise, practise.
e) The athletes need to follow a rigorous training schedule.

Exercise D

Athletes keep <u>getting</u> better every year with the improvement of <u>training</u> facilities and equipment. <u>Existing</u> world records are broken on a regular basis. Many athletes, desperate <u>to win</u> the glory of the gold, turn to <u>performance-enhancing</u> drugs, such as steroids and other forms of what the athletes hope will be untraceable drugs. Regular drug <u>testing</u> of athletes is now a requirement in the highly competitive world of athletics. The number of records that have been awarded to athletes who have managed <u>to slip</u> by the <u>testing</u> is unclear. However, what remains a little-changed fact is the average age of <u>top-performing</u> athletes. In the early 1900s, the average age of gold medal winners was 25. Today, this average has changed only slightly to 24.6. This indicates that no matter what athletes do <u>to improve</u> their <u>training</u>, equipment, or performance, age will probably be the most influential factor.

Possible answers:

1. ...to win gold.
2. Taking performance-enhancing drugs...
3. ...to win at any cost.
4. ...to test for drug usage.
5. ...being caught.

Exercise E

Answers will vary.

Writing

Exercise A

Paragraph 3

Exercise B

1. last sentence
2. attention grabber
3. Mike Tyson incident
4. Persuasive
5. such behaviour cannot be tolerated

Exercise C

Answers will vary.

Academic Word List

Exercise A

1. d
2. h
3. g
4. f
5. i
6. j
7. b
8. a
9. c
10. e
11. p
12. s
13. l
14. n
15. r
16. t
17. k
18. m
19. q
20. o

Exercise B

1. ac / a / **děm** / ic
2. a / **chǐeve**
3. a / **nǎl** / y / sis
4. **ǎn** / nu / al
5. **ǎs** / pect
6. com / **mǐt** / ment
7. con / cen / **trǎ** /tion
8. **děm** / on / strate
9. es / **tǎb** / lished
10. fi / **nǎn** / cial
11. **fǒ** / cuš
12. **ǐn** / ju / ry
13. pro / **fěs** / sion / al
14. reg / u / **lǎ** / tions
15. re / **quǐred**
16. se / **lěct**
17. **sǔb** / se / quent
18. sym / **bǒl** / ic
19. **těch** / ni / cal
20. tra / **dǐ** / tion / al

Exercise C

1. (n) academy   (adv) academically
2. (n) achievement / achiever   (adj) achievable
3. (v) analyze   (adj) analytic   (adv) analytically
4. (adv) annually
5. (v) commit   (adj) committed
6. (v) concentrate   (adj) concentrated
7. (n) demonstration / demonstrator   (adj) demonstrative / demonstrated / demonstrable
   (adv) demonstrably / demonstratively
8. (n) establishment   (v) establish

9. (n) finances / financier (v) finance   (adv) financially
10. (n) focus
11. (v) injure   (adj) injured
12. (n) profession / professionalism   (adv) professionally
13. (v) regulate   (adj) (un/de) regulated
14. (n) requirement / requisition   (v) require
15. (n) selection   (adj) selective   (adv) selectively
16. (n) symbol / symbolism   (v) symbolize
    (adv) symbolically
17. (n) technique   (adv) technically
18. (n) tradition / traditionalist   (adv) traditionally

Exercise D

Answers will vary.

Exercise E

1. demonstrated
2. commitment
3. achievable
4. established
5. professional
6. focused
7. technical
8. injury
9. concentrate
10. aspects
11. symbol
12. regulated
13. regulations
14. subsequently
15. financial
16. annual
17. academies
18. selected
19. analysis
20. traditional
21. non-traditional

Unit 9

Exercise A

1. impulsive
2. perished
3. atmospheric
4. unique
5. onslaught
6. interloper
7. tread
8. government
9. diversify
10. entice

Exercise B

A. Things that relate to **regulated**.
B. Things that relate to **synthetic**.
C. Things that relate to **cultivation**.
D. Things that relate to **fertilizer**.
E. Things that relate to **optimal**.
F. Things that relate to **wholesome**.

Exercise C

1. urban
2. organic
3. antioxidants
4. residual
5. healthier
6. organizations
7. standards
8. sustaining
9. depletion
10. genetically
11. synthetic
12. compost
13. fertilizers
14. rotate
15. condition

Exercise D

1. False. No food causes pimples; they are caused by genetics and stress.
2. True. Studies show that chicken soup makes your nose run which helps you get the cold germs out of your system.
3. False. Wearing garlic has no practical value except to maybe keep everyone away from you because of the smell.
4. True. Steaks are cold and flexible—the cold reduces the swelling and constricts broken blood vessels, and the flexibility allows them to conform to the face.
5. True. Ginger and crackers both absorb acids in the stomach.
6. True. Your body burns the energy from food within four hours. After a long night's sleep, your body needs food to function well.

7. True. The vitamin A in carrots helps maintain eye tissue.
8. False. The colour of eggshell depends on the type of hen and has no effect on nutrition.
9. False. Two or three healthful snacks between meals benefit children who have high energy needs.
10. False. The alternatives do not contain any significant amount of vitamins or minerals.

Exercise E

Answers will vary.

Exercise A

1. well-known
2. fat-reduced
3. processed
4. introduced
5. well-trained
6. proven
7. frequently mentioned
8. disappointed
9. prepackaged
10. hidden

Exercise B

1. Top athletes follow carefully planned diets.
2. Organically grown fruit is more expensive.
3. Carefully controlled product placement influences our purchases.
4. Locally grown produce is seldom sold at your local supermarket.
5. The televised debate on eating organic food was insightful.
6. Carefully controlled food prices ensure large profits for corporations.

Exercise C

organically grown
contained
packed
designed
recognized
detailed
processed
confined
enhanced
certified

Exercise D

1. concerned
2. approved / processed
3. established
4. clarified / informed
5. standardized
6. influenced
7. faced
8. utilized

Exercise E

1. descriptor of subject
2. pre-modifier / pre-modifier
3. pre-modifier
4. pre-modifier / pre-modifier
5. pre-modifier
6. post-modifier
7. post-modifier
8. post-modifier

Exercise F

Answers will vary.

Vocabulary Expansion

Exercise A

Possible answers:

Suffix	Word	Root Word	Meaning or Function of Suffix
-ly	elegantly traditionally nearly definitely recently	elegant traditional near definite recent	- in the stated way
-ion	invasion creation obsession	invade create obsess	- shows action or condition - forms a noun
-er	rarer older researcher simpler	rare old research simple	- forms the comparative - person who is connected or involved with
-al	national	nation	- connected with
-y	healthy	health	- like the stated thing (root word) - forms an adjective when added to noun
-ful	hopeful	hope	- full of

Note: traditionally has two suffixes (tradition + al + ly)

Exercise B

suffix	noun	verb	adjective	adverb
-ly			recent organic complete tight federal	recently organically completely tightly federally
	ease necessity simplicity chemical	necessitate	easy necessary simple chemical	easily necessarily simply chemically
-tion	production consumption	produce consume	produced consuming	
-al	nature		natural	naturally
-er	buyer consumer	buy consume	consuming consummate	

Exercise C

Possible answers:

select: selected, selection, selective, selectively, selectivity, selectiveness, selector

nature: naturally, natural, naturalize

taste: tasteless, taster, tasty, tasteful, tastefully, tastelessly

consume: consumables, consumer, consumerism, consuming, consumption

Exercise D

Answers will vary.

Writing

Exercises A through E

Answers will vary.

Academic Word List

Exercise A

1. categories
2. data
3. layer
4. stress
5. trend
6. design
7. decline
8. process
9. range
10. shift
11. purchase
12. expansion
13. corporate
14. technology
15. consumer
16. percent
17. location
18. acquisition
19. pursue
20. conduct

Exercise B

1. ac / qui / **si** / tion
2. **cat** / e /go / ries
3. **con** / duct
4. con/ **sum** / er
5. **cor** / po / rate
6. **da** / ta
7. de / **cline**
8. de / **sign**
9. ex / **pan** / sion
10. **lay** / er
11. lo / **ca** / tion
12. per / **cent**
13. **proc** / ess
14. **pur** / chase
15. pur / **sue**
16. **range**
17. **shift**
18. **stress**
19. tech / **nol** / o / gy
20. **trend**

Exercise C

1. (v) acquire   (adj) acquired
2. (v) categorize
3. (v) conduct
4. (v) consume   (adj) consumable / consuming
5. (n) corporation
6. (adj) declining
7. (v) design
8. (v) expand   (adj) expansive / expanding
9. (adj) layered
10. (v) (re)locate
11. (n) percentage
12. (v) process   (adj) (un)processed
13. (adj) purchased
14. (n) pursuit   (adj) pursued
15. (adj) shifting
16. (adj) stressed / stressful
17. (adj) technological   (adv) technologically
18. (adj) trendy

Exercise D

Answers will vary.

Exercise E

1. corporations
2. consumer
3. trends
4. shifts
5. decline
6. expanding
7. conduct
8. acquire
9. purchased
10. technology
11. data
12. locate
13. design
14. categorized
15. layered
16. processed
17. percentage
18. stress
19. range
20. pursue

Unit 10

Vocabulary

Exercise A

1. What is *retirement*?
2. What is a *decade*?
3. What is a *stage*?
4. What is an *identity*?
5. What is *an adolescent*?
6. What is *puberty*?
7. What is *revolutionize*?
8. What is *mature*?
9. What is *fertile*?
10. What is *longevity*?

Exercises B and C

Answers will vary.

Grammar Focus

Exercise A

1. Incorrect: plays
2. Incorrect: took on
3. Incorrect: has been criticized
4. Incorrect: will no longer target
5. Correct
6. Incorrect: will likely have lived
7. Incorrect: deteriorate
8. Correct

Exercise B

1. develop
2. were developing / developed
3. have been developing
4. have just developed / just developed
5. is developing / has been developing
6. developed
7. will be developing
8. will have developed / will be developing
9. develop / will develop
10. had already been developing / was already developing / had already developed

Exercise C

Note: Verb forms are listed below. Sentences will vary.

1. will be retiring
2. will identify
3. was / were developing
4. has / have been maturing
5. am / is / are coaching
6. span(s)
7. will have identified
8. matured

9. had expected
10. will have been giving
11. will have revolutionized
12. had been expecting

Vocabulary Expansion

Exercise A

Answers will vary.

Exercise B

impact on / of
limit on / to
stages of / in
policy on / about
opportunity for / in / to

Exercise C

Answers will vary.

Grammar Expansion

Exercise A

1. Critical work in this field was done at the turn of the 19th century by Sigmund Freud, a trained physician, ...
2. But a study of literacy rates among different generational groups in Canada revealed...
   ...fewer people in **earlier generations** had access to education.
   ...who **a few decades ago** would never have been included in mainstream education...
3. People want to be in control of their own lives—that's only natural.

Exercise B

1. was
2. can't believe
3. flies
4. saw
5. had
6. are
7. doesn't look
8. saw
9. look
10. is
11. looks
12. seems
13. announced
14. was
15. does the time go / has the time gone
16. was
17. won
18. will be
19. do you believe / can you believe

20. married / got married
21. was
22. worked / were working
23. will marry
24. leave

Exercise C

1. was
2. had accepted
3. gave
4. had
5. tried
6. disliked
7. picked
8. tasted
9. said
10. stand
11. suppose
12. don't know
13. don't you go
14. have tasted / taste
15. eat
16. will never want
17. forgave
18. consented
19. arrived
20. took
21. was / had been
22. must be
23. said
24. rest
25. will bring
26. brought
27. thought
28. wanted
29. had
30. heard
31. saw
32. ran
33. found
34. stood / was standing
35. made
36. could get
37. said
38. have
39. are

Exercises D and E

Answers will vary.

Writing

Exercise A

Possible answers:
1. Town mouse visits his cousin in the country
2. Mice eat country-type food

3. Town mouse doesn't like country-type food, and invites country mouse to the city
4. Country mouse goes to the city
5. Town mouse takes the country mouse to eat a fancy meal
6. Country mouse loves the meal
7. Things become dangerous
8. Country mouse wants to go home

Exercises B and C

Answers will vary.

Academic Word List

Exercise A

1. impact
2. commissioned
3. significant
4. participants
5. definition
6. psychological
7. policy
8. conference
9. administration
10. available
11. environments
12. attitude
13. a contract
14. principal
15. identified
16. series
17. institution
18. maximum
19. period
20. similar

Exercise B

1. ad / min / i / **strå** / tion
2. **åt** / ti / tudes
3. a / **vail** / a / ble
4. com / **mis** / sion
5. **con** / fer / ence
6. **con** / tract
7. de / fi / **ni** / tion
8. en / **vi** / ron / ment
9. i / **dèn** / ti / fied
10. **im** / pact
11. **in** / sti / tute
12. **max** / i / mum
13. par / ti / ci / **på** / tion
14. **pe** / ri / od
15 **po** / li / cy
16. **prin** / ci / pal
17. psy / **chò** / lo / gy
18. **sè** / ries
19. sig / **ni** / fi / cant
20. **si** / mi / lar

Exercise C

1. (v) administer   (adj) administrative
   (adv) administratively
2. (n) availability
3. (v) commission   (adj) commissioned
4. (v) conference   (adj) conference
5. (v) contract   (adj) contractual
6. (v) define
7. (adj) environmental   (adv) environmentally
8. (n) identification   (adj) identifiable
9. (v) impact   (adj) impactful
10. (n) institution
11. (v) maximize
12. (v) participate   (adj) participatory; participative
13. (adj) periodic   (adv) periodically
14. (adj) psychological   (adv) psychologically
15. (adj) serial
16. (n) significance   (adv) significantly
17. (n) similarity   (adv) similarly

5. commissioned
6. psychology
7. environments
8. similar
9. principal
10. policies
11. period
12. administrators
13. impact
14. participation
15. maximum
16. series
17. contracts
18. conferences
19. identified
20. available

Exercise D

Answers will vary.

Exercise E

1. defined
2. significant
3. attitudes
4. institutes

Credits

Literary Credits

12/13 (Exercise B clues) Excerpts from *Ghosts and the Supernatural* (Collins, 1989) by Pam Beasant.

16/17 "A Cradle of Love" from *An Angel to Watch Over Me* by Joan Webster Anderson. Copyright © 1994 by Joan Webster Anderson.

63 Morris, Charles G; Maisto, Albert, *Understanding Psychology*, 8th Edition © 2008, p.242. Adapted by permission of Pearson Education, Inc., Upper Saddle River, NJ.

72/73 "What is Reality TV?" copyright *The Age*

74/75 by Declan Reilly a writer at Helium.com

79/80 "Girls and Gaming" adapted from Agosto, D. (2003). http://girlstech.douglass.rutgers.edu/PDF/GirlsAndGaming.pdf

Photograph Credits

5 Artwork © by Phil Testemale

7 iStock Photo/Heather Mason Design

19 Genevieve Sang, gensang@gmail.com

25 Gloria McPherson-Ramirez

26 (1) Carnaval de Québec; (2) Catherine Antonin/iStock International Inc; (3) Rafael Laguillo/Big Stock Photo; (4) Yang Xiaofeng/Big Stock Photo; (5) Antoine Beyeler/Big Stock Photo

33 Ryan LeBaron/Big Stock Photo

40 Genevieve Sang, gensang@gmail.com

63 Jeff Metzger/iStock International Inc

109 *Composition through Pictures*, J.B. Heaton, Pearson Education Limited, 1966.